Conor Woodman is an inves...
journalist, BBC reporter and...
maker. He has reported from...
parts of the world on topics ranging
from gangs and organised crime to
slavery and smuggling. He is the
author of the critically acclaimed
books *The Adventure Capitalist*,
Unfair Trade, which was shortlisted
for the Orwell Prize, and *The Scam Hunter*. Conor was
the presenter of National Geographic Channel's *Scam
City* and ITV's *Exposure: Britain's Booming Cannabis
Business*.

METH ROAD

*A life-and-death investigation following the world's
most destructive narcotic to Australia*

METH
ROAD

CONOR WOODMAN

ALLEN&UNWIN
SYDNEY · MELBOURNE · AUCKLAND · LONDON

First published in 2023

Allen & Unwin
Cammeraygal Country
83 Alexander Street
Crows Nest NSW 2065
Australia
Phone: (61 2) 8425 0100
Email: info@allenandunwin.com
Web: www.allenandunwin.com

Allen & Unwin acknowledges the Traditional Owners of the Country on which we live and work. We pay our respects to all Aboriginal and Torres Strait Islander Elders, past and present.

A catalogue record for this book is available from the National Library of Australia

NATIONAL LIBRARY OF AUSTRALIA

ISBN 978 1 76087 855 9

Map by Mika Tabata
Author photograph by Jack Laurence
Except where otherwise stated, photographs are from the author's collection
Set in 12/16 pt Sabon LT Pro by Midland Typesetters, Australia
Printed and bound in Australia by the Opus Group

10 9 8 7 6 5 4 3 2 1

MIX
Paper | Supporting responsible forestry
FSC® C001695
www.fsc.org

The paper in this book is FSC® certified. FSC® promotes environmentally responsible, socially beneficial and economically viable management of the world's forests.

CONTENTS

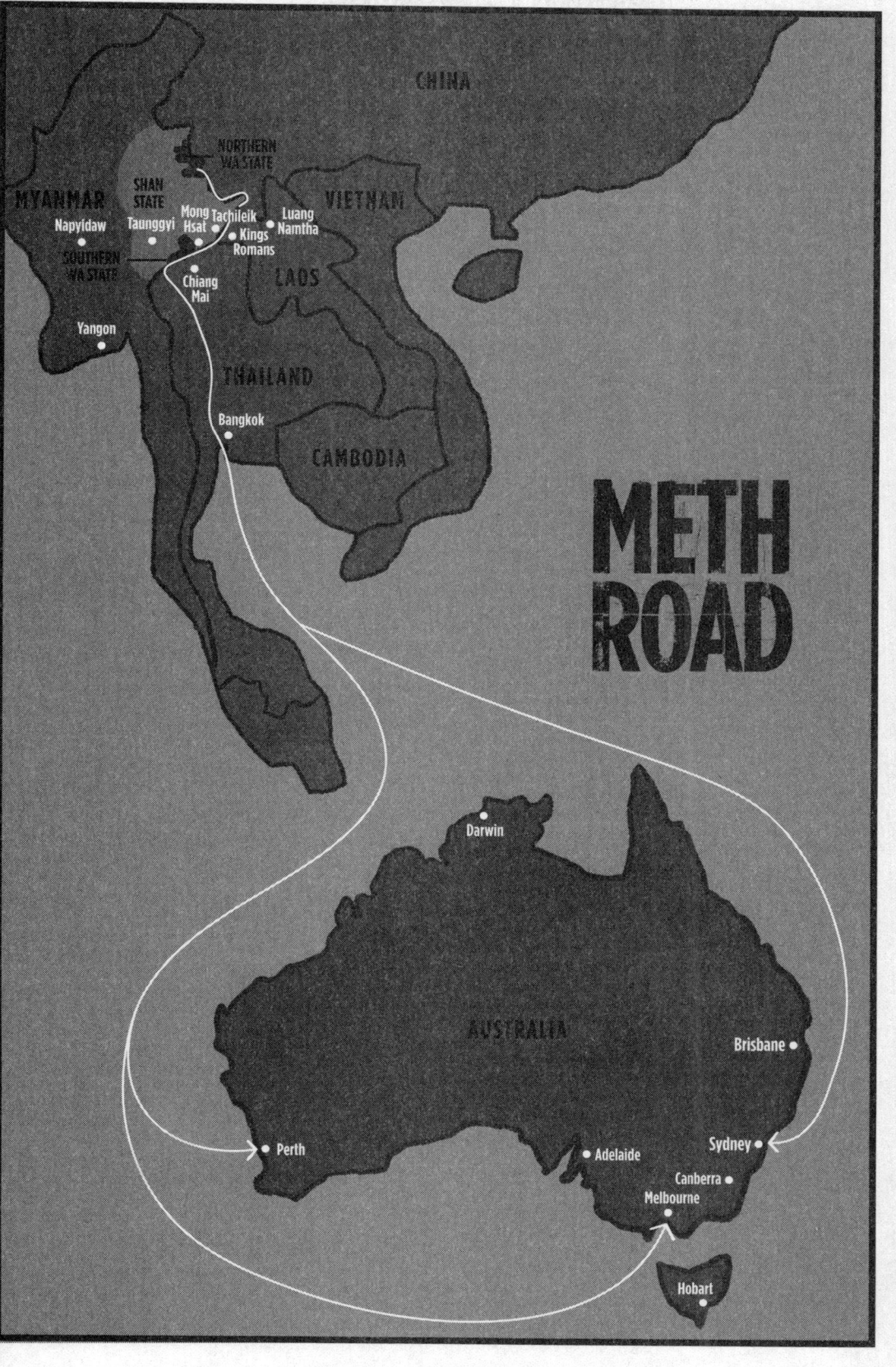

PROLOGUE

WELCOME TO THE JUNGLE

We're driving deeper into the jungle. I have a t-shirt tied tightly over my head so that I can't see where we're going. I'm anxious, not because I'm disorientated but because I've had to hand over my phone. I hate the feeling that I can't contact anyone. The man sitting up front in the vehicle insisted I give it to him on account of the GPS tracking that's built into it. Now he's removed the SIM card and says he'll hold on to it until we return to the town we've just left. He is clear that his priority is, first and foremost, that I will never be able to recreate this journey, never be able to locate the place he and his colleagues are about to show me.

Inside this sweaty blindfold, my mind drifts back to a morning a couple of years before. It was the morning when this whole journey started, although I didn't realise that at the time. I was sitting at a friend's kitchen table in Los Angeles eating pancakes when my phone pinged with a WhatsApp message. It was from a TV producer I knew who lived in Bangkok.

I've worked all over South-East Asia, mostly on stories revolving around crime and drugs, and I still have friends and colleagues dotted around who stay in touch. This particular friend was now working for a major US TV network on a series about drugs. The American director of the episode she was producing wanted to film inside a 'real meth lab'. My friend's message explained that two nights earlier she'd crossed over the border from Thailand into Shan State, Myanmar, to meet a criminal informant (CI) who was promising to help make the necessary introductions to get access. Her next message was a little more alarming.

'Switch to Signal,' the message said. 'Things here are fucked up.'

Signal is an encrypted message service that can be set up so that every time you send a message, it can be read for only a few seconds before it's deleted from your phone and every server everywhere, so that nobody can ever read it again. It's what people use if they think someone might be listening in to a conversation—as I guess they might be if you're doing a story about meth labs in Shan State.

I didn't know much about Shan State back then, other than it was one of the most dangerous places on earth. I knew that Myanmar, or Burma as it was once called, had been at war with itself for sixty years, ever since the military overthrew the government and declared a junta. Looking at a map, you'll see right away that Myanmar is mostly impenetrable jungle, divided up into several semi-autonomous states. A couple of those states to the east, Shan State and Wa State in particular, never much liked the idea of being ruled by the government in the capital, Naypyidaw, and rebelled. The Shan and the Wa people have been at war with each other and the central government ever since.

But waging war is an expensive pursuit. It's long been thought that the armies fighting the Myanmar government— including the Shan State Army and the United Wa State Army—have funded their efforts by selling drugs. Drugs buy guns, guns shoot enemies, and internal civil war rages.

The other thing I knew is that CIs in the drug world are often crooks and addicts themselves, and that means they are unpredictable. When you're working with a CI, you have to keep an eye on them constantly, and you have to be prepared for them to flake out on you. It's frustrating if it happens in your town, or a place you know well, but if you're in a war zone where people are jumpy as hell and life is cheap, then it can really put you on edge.

My friend explained that she had been meant to rendezvous with her CI that morning in a village deep in Shan territory but his body had been discovered by the Thai DEA—Thailand's Drug Enforcement Administration—in a border raid. She had good links to the Thai DEA and one of the officers had been kind enough to let her know that 'her boy' had been coldly executed. He sent her a photo as proof. When she forwarded the photo to me, it put me right off my pancakes.

The picture showed a young man whose life had been ended abruptly with a single gunshot to the head. He was now lying on the ground next to two huge piles of drugs, what looked to me like a couple of hundred kilos of 'ice'—high-grade crystal methamphetamine—and a few million 'yaba', or speed pills. In the background of the shot, I could see half a dozen smiling DEA agents, who all looked thrilled with the bust. Whatever the CI had done, he'd been in the wrong place at the wrong time.

I'm happy to say that my friend made it out of Shan okay that day. But back across the border in Thailand, everyone from the American TV network she was working for was freaked out. The producers back in New York pulled the story, deciding that going into Shan again was too dangerous. For the time being, the secrets of Shan's jungle meth labs would remain just that—secrets.

———

On the other hand, I had my own ideas. I began to read more and more about Myanmar. I became fascinated with how exactly a war had continued to rage in the jungles of an underdeveloped country fuelled by the profits of the international drug trade. I became increasingly curious about why so much of that money was flowing in from Australia, a country that has no obvious historical or cultural links to Myanmar.

I decided to find out more about how exactly the connections had been made, to look into who the major players were, how the production was coordinated and what sums of money were being made. What started to emerge was that two countries, geographically distant and with so little shared history, had become the start and end points of an 10,000-kilometre road linking jungle-based insurgents with new world drug addicts.

I decided that I would do exactly the opposite of what the US TV network had done. I resolved to go where they had not. I resolved to travel through Australia to meet the people whose lives and livelihoods were made along the Meth Road, then to follow it to Thailand, Laos and eventually Myanmar to see for myself how things linked together.

Over what should have been the next twelve months but ended up, thanks to a global pandemic, taking nearly three years, I immersed myself in the world of methamphetamine. Several trips to Asia and a tour of Australia's eastern and central regions have enabled me to get a picture of how methamphetamine impacts the lives of real people. I've conducted scores of interviews with meth producers, dealers and consumers, as well as people whose legitimate livelihoods are conducted in meth's peripheral industries such as law enforcement, addiction treatment and media coverage.

At times, my journey along the Meth Road has been exhausting and frustrating but the people I have met have all been generous enough to share their time and their stories with me. I've tried my best to represent them as honestly and fairly as possible. They don't always agree with each other, and if I've learned anything it's that there are many different views on methamphetamine and what to do about it. But I've listened to all these views and considered them with an open mind before forming my own.

It's important to say that the opinions that I express here in *Meth Road* are very much my own. I'm sure some will criticise me as a non-Australian, asking what right I have to make judgements about something that is not happening where I live. 'Go and write a book about cocaine in London, mate,' they might legitimately say, and maybe one day I will. But for now, this is where I've focused my attention. In my defence, I believe that having less skin in the game, being an outsider to the issue, actually gives me an advantage—a fresh pair of eyes, an unbiased look at what is going on. I hope that might allow me to throw up some fresh ideas.

I've chosen to begin the book in Australia because that is where you, the reader, are most likely to be located. But from there, the narrative shifts to Asia because that is where the Meth Road begins. I want to take you back, following meth's path from user to distributor all the way to the source, one step at a time, meeting the people I met as I worked backwards to discover where it was coming from and how it was getting to Australia.

Once we've uncovered some of the secrets of Asia's meth trade, we return to Australia to find out how the drug is affecting society, hearing from the people whose lived experiences best describe it. There are broadly four pillars to Australia's 'drug strategy'—supply reduction, demand reduction, drug treatment and harm reduction. I have explored each of these to interrogate what I believe to be the substantive questions.

At the time of writing, the situation in Australia is dire. Meth usage, which dipped briefly during the Covid pandemic, has risen again to pre-pandemic levels. More than 9 tonnes of methamphetamine were consumed in Australia in 2022; 500 people died from taking meth and another 12,400 people were hospitalised. Just when the need for rehabilitation has never been higher, the country's ability to provide it is at breaking point. Waiting lists are so long that addiction centres are turning away new applicants. St Vincent's Hospital in Sydney, one of the nation's leading drug-rehabilitation centres, has a waiting list of more than 100 people.

In the end, I want to create a manifesto for progress, a to-do list that I think could help improve the impact that meth is having on society in Australia. During my time travelling through the country, I felt a strong sense that most Australians wanted some sort of change. The situation has become intolerable to many, and yet, time and again, I found myself asking, 'What exactly is it that Australia wants?'

I found myself asking a similar question that morning in the Myanmar jungle, bumping along in the back of an SUV. 'What exactly is it that *I* want?' That was when I realised the answer was there in front of me. I was in exactly the place that I wanted to be, blindfolded in the jungle by Burmese gangsters, following the trail deeper into the forest, on a journey to discover where the Meth Road ended. This was when things finally made some sense.

PART ONE

SUPPLY

1

SHAKE AND BAKE

I'm following Vix, a local drug dealer down a backstreet in a rundown suburb on the Gold Coast in Queensland. As a condition of our 'agreement', I have consented to withhold enough description to prevent anyone from guessing our location. Suffice to say that the house at which we stop is a rather tatty-looking bungalow on a street of similarly tatty bungalows that wouldn't draw anyone's attention.

I had met Vix a few days before at a homeless shelter in Southport, Queensland, where volunteers were handing out a free lunch to rough sleepers. She immediately stood out as someone who knew everyone, and I watched her stopping and chatting with regulars and newcomers alike. It didn't take long to see that she was working the room, making it known she was *holding*, pushing bags containing 'points'—0.1 grams of ice, or crystal meth-amphetamine—to her customers for $60 a pop.

Outside the shelter, I caught up with her as she was squirrelling away a roll of cash in her pocket, a wide-eyed happy customer scurrying off up the street to fix. With so many dependent users among Australia's homeless community, the soup kitchen was the perfect gathering place for a drug dealer to conduct business. We started to talk and she said that once she'd completed her deals for the day, I should come back inside with her for a cup of tea.

I'll return to her again later but for now what's important is that while we were drinking that cup of tea, she mentioned a contact who sometimes supplied her with ice. When I asked if I could meet him, she told me there might be a way. After she made a call, she confirmed that I could go and see him as long as I paid *the going rate*, which meant that I could engage his services for a fee.

'But it's not for everyone,' she warned, as I handed her $1000.

Hours later, I'm being led up an overgrown path, where rusty and rotting children's toys are littered across a small lawn. The bungalow's weathered front door opens and a tall, drawn-looking man with bright-blue eyes and a heavy moustache eyes me suspiciously before he invites me inside. The dealer waves goodbye; this is as far as she will go. I step inside a narrow, dimly lit hallway and the man locks the door behind me, watching the dealer leave through the glass.

'You got crocodiles, you got sharks, you've got the inland taipan that lives on the east coast, and which will kill you in eleven seconds,' he says, rather cryptically. 'But the most dangerous thing in Australia is Australian women.'

I follow him along the corridor as he laughs at his own joke. I have been told to call him Chris, though I suspect that is not his real name. For the duration of this book, I have used aliases when they've been given to me, and I've changed the names and identities of anyone I believe could be arrested or harmed as a result of talking with me. Other than that, their stories are told as I heard them, and I hope you'll find that their real names are far less important than what they have to say.

I've decided to start my journey in Queensland because, believe it or not, this is where I believe the history of Australia's relationship with the highest purity form of methamphetamine, what we now know as ice, all began. We'll get into that unusual story but before that, I want to tell you about Chris because what Chris does inside this bungalow represents the current state of play.

At the back of the house, we walk into a small lean-to kitchen, where Chris points to my shirt—my cue to unbutton myself. Years of making undercover television programs have made certain people wary of me and so, before we can proceed, he wants me to reveal that I am not wearing any secret recording devices. Happy that I'm clean, he nods that I can do myself back up again.

Chris is all wiry and sinewy, his skin is tanned and his forearms are heavily tattooed. Those blue eyes almost glow in the dim light of the shabby kitchen. It's hard to guess his age—he has a head of thick hair and he's dressed in jeans and a t-shirt that all suggests he's younger than he looks. I'd guess forty but, as with a lot of heavy meth users, I could be out by ten years.

Chris locks the kitchen door, which makes me a little nervous. That's not because Chris is a criminal who is likely to pull a gun on me—though he might. Nor because I particularly worry about being locked in rooms with criminals—I'm actually pretty used to that. No, I'm a little anxious because Chris's particular brand of criminality comes with a health warning. What Chris does for a living, the reason that I'm here, could kill both of us. Because Chris is a methamphetamine 'cook'.

My $1000 to engage Chris's 'services' means that he's going to teach me how to make a batch of meth. I'm never going to make a batch of meth but what I am going to do is describe the process to you in gory, blow-by-blow detail. Chris offers this unusual service to would-be amateur cooks who are keen to learn for themselves how to produce crystal methamphetamine. Like a cookery class for drug dealers. If he is to be believed, then by the time I leave this house I will know how to make up to 20 grams of methamphetamine using products and chemicals that are freely available in the shops of any town in Australia.

———

Twenty grams of product is below the level at which a lab is considered to be 'commercial' by Australian police services. Hundreds of clandestine laboratories, known as clan labs, are discovered every year in Australia, and the police use the same categories provided by the United

Nations Office on Drugs and Crime in their data. Full definitions of the four categories—addict-based, other small-scale, medium-scale and industrial-scale—are mainly determined by the size of output and the equipment used. Essentially, the first two categories are labs that produce less than 500 grams, while the last two produce from 500 grams to many kilos of output.

There was a substantial increase in the number of clandestine laboratories raided in Australia in the second half of the 1990s. In New South Wales, for example, there were barely any labs discovered in 1990, then around 100 in 1997–98, and by 2002–03 that number was 340. The picture was the same around the country. The number of clandestine laboratories detected in Australia more than doubled during this period; however, the majority of clandestine laboratory detections occurred in Queensland.

In 1994, the unbridled and exponential explosion in clandestine meth labs in Queensland led the Queensland Police to enlist the help of a forensic chemist, Peter Vallely. Within twelve months of his appointment, Vallely's workload suddenly increased. The scientist from Queensland started to see more and more home-cooked meth appearing in his lab.

Vallely decided to put police officers through chemistry lessons specifically tailored to educate them on how to make meth. The theory was that if officers understood how the criminals were operating, they'd be better at spotting the signs and clues that would lead to further arrests.

Vallely even built his own meth lab within the police department's buildings where he could show cops how to cook meth with everyday chemicals. He tried as far as he could to copy the techniques that he was seeing criminal gangs employ to make the meth that was turning up in their busts. He wanted officers to understand that meth labs don't always look like traditional laboratories. Under the eyes of a skilled cook, meth could be prepared using any number of different methods.

Police officers loved their chemistry classes with Vallely. They were keen to know what they were dealing with once a bust had been made; increasingly, they were walking into highly toxic environments, filled with chemicals and reagents that they didn't understand and that could potentially harm them. It wasn't just a case of catching the bad guys. It was about protecting themselves and the wider community from harm.

When Vallely built his first meth lab, the method that he used was the same as that being widely used by clandestine cooks across Australia—what was known as the red phosphorus method. Cooks had to know what they were doing because red phosphorus, which is widely used in fireworks, is potentially very explosive. The cook would mix red phosphorus with ephedrine and hydriodic acid, then heat, filter and crystallise it. A decent cook could turn 50 to 75 per cent of the ephedrine used into meth, which was usually a kind of orangey-brown colour. The whole process took two or three days.

'It wasn't for amateurs,' Vallely says. 'Criminal gangs were using cooks, who were looked after as a bit of a prize.'

But then, in 1996, everything changed. Suddenly, Vallely started to see high-purity methamphetamine with a white crystalline appearance appearing all over Australia. In one year, police saw a fourfold explosion in the number of clan labs in Queensland alone. These new labs were different from the red phosphorus labs. They were smaller, had less kit and, crucially, used different chemicals.

The method of synthesis had completely changed overnight. It needed less equipment and it turned over a fresh batch of meth in under two hours. All the kit you needed for a functional, medium-sized lab could be carried inside a single cardboard box. This gave rise to a new term—the 'box lab'.

Vallely was dumbfounded. There are many, many ways to make meth and yes, that information has always been freely available to the public. You can find it all out on the internet now, but back then, it was only detailed in the scientific literature.

'The sources I would use to understand these processes were exactly the same as I'd use if I was a cook thinking, "Well, I can't buy that ingredient anymore. What else could I use?"' Vallely says. 'A cook and I could be sitting side by side in the university library thumbing through the same journal.'

It's a funny image, but in fact, the cook who changed everything was no university student. The inventor of the box lab was an uneducated meth user who'd grown up on the southern Queensland coast. The reason for the sudden and profound proliferation of meth labs across the country was down to one young man who had made a discovery that would go on to change the face of meth production around the world. His name was Dale Francis Drake.

Dale was the oldest of six siblings of a hard-working, blue-collar Queensland family from Hervey Bay. His brothers and sisters would grow up to have good jobs and become solid members of the community—a teacher, a trawlerman and a builder. As kids, their father would take them at weekends to the beach to fish. There was nothing out of the ordinary about the Drakes except perhaps that the eldest child, Dale, was particularly nerdy, singled out at school as a kid with enormous potential.

'He was always a bright kid,' his sister Neta tells me. 'He should have gone on to be a doctor or a professor.'

Neta says that her big brother always had his nose in a book and was curious about everything, unlike the other boys who'd mostly be out surfing or kicking a footy. Dale was maybe hindered in that regard as he was diagnosed with diabetes. He was in and out of hospital, more than once experiencing the terrifying trauma of falling into a life-threatening coma.

Then Dale got into meth. As a diabetic, he was already comfortable injecting himself, and very quickly he progressed from smoking to shooting meth into his veins. His family did not approve, so Dale moved away from Hervey Bay, relocating to Gympie where there was more of a drug 'scene' in which he felt comfortable.

In between bouts of addiction, Neta says Dale took up several casual jobs, working variously in a mine, on a trawler and in a power station. It's not clear where he first got access to the kind of chemicals with which he would revolutionise meth production, but somehow he came up with a way of cooking meth that was unique.

Wherever the inspiration came from, Dale's 'hypo method' of producing meth, which would become synonymous worldwide with the box lab, was a stroke of genius because it didn't require the cook to have access to red phosphorus. Instead, the key ingredient, ephedrine, could be turned into meth using a combination of liquid iodine and hypophosphorous acid, which was widely used in a bunch of different industries.

Julian is a long-serving Queensland police officer and has agreed to speak to me if I change his name. He's not the first serving official to make this request and, while I am respecting his wishes, I have to point out that it's been quite revealing how many drug users have been happy for me to use their real names while drug prosecutors prefer to speak anonymously.

In any case, Julian has worked for a forensic crime team within the Queensland Police for more than thirty years and remembers well the emergence of Dale's method early in his career. He says it had everyone in his team scratching their heads. Out of nowhere, an explosion of high-quality methamphetamine hit the streets, but rather than coming from a single point, it was coming from all over the state.

'We went from busting three labs a year, which all used the red phosphorus production method, to all of a sudden, hundreds of these pseudoephedrine labs popping up,' he says. 'These ones were using hypophosphorous acid, Sudafed and iodine.'

This was Dale's signature recipe. For ten grand, in much the same way as Chris is teaching me now, Dale was selling other people the know-how needed to cook meth using his method. His students could make that money back pretty quickly if they did it right. Dale was also providing all the kit and ingredients they needed for their first cook in a single box, hence the 'box lab'.

Julian says that to target the box labs, the Queensland Police focused on where the ingredients were coming from. Sudafed was available in every pharmacy in Australia, while iodine was an unrestricted item you could buy over the counter. Julian and his team decided to focus on hypophosphorous acid, which was being widely used for glass etching all over Queensland. Meth cooks were evidently bribing people in the glass industry to slip them bottles of the acid on the side.

The Australian government had already begun to regulate the sale of red phosphorus so that only companies who could prove that they had a legitimate use for it could get it. 'I own a meth lab' didn't qualify as a reason. But because nobody before Dale had thought of using hypophosphorous acid, you could still get it without any additional paperwork.

The other benefit of Dale's 'hypo' production method was that the final product contained so much less contaminating material that had to be removed by additional chemical processes. As long as you did a clean job of the main reaction, the product that came out at the end was pretty close to what you could put in your pipe and smoke. It also drastically reduced the time for synthesis. Cooks didn't need to supervise a bubbling flask for days on end, during which time something could catch fire or the police could kick your door in. Now they could turn chemicals into meth in a couple of hours.

There were downsides, though, the main one being that you needed a specialist kit. A reaction flask, a condenser and a reliable heat source were things that had to be sourced from technical retailers. But once you had everything you needed, then you could knock out 50 to 100 grams of meth every time. For a competent cook who could stick to the recipe, it was a licence to print money.

A cruel irony for the man who enabled so many others around the world to make millions and millions of dollars was that Dale never made any real money himself. He died aged forty, poor and addicted to meth, his diabetes severely exacerbated by his drug use. The meth he was injecting put undue strain on his already clapped-out kidneys and it's likely the toxic fumes he was exposing himself to inside his home lab added further insult to injury.

But Dale was never caught either, never arrested, never did jail time. His discovery only came to light years after his death. But its significance endured. Neta says that not long ago, she bumped into an old school friend who was working for the Australian Border Force. 'She was a bit off with me,' Neta says. 'Then she told me that the training there still includes a whole section on Dale and how he was this "master criminal".'

Years after Dale's death, Brisbane's daily paper, *The Courier-Mail*, ran a hatchet piece on him. It described him as a 'hillbilly satanist,' which doesn't tally with the reality of a man who had the intellect, however misplaced, to change the way methamphetamine was being made not only in Australia but around the world. Neta wrote to the editor of *The Courier-Mail* on behalf of her family, asking for the paper to print a retraction and an apology. She never received a reply.

She says that far from being a criminal mastermind, Dale was often approached by gangs, including bikie gangs, who wanted him to come and work exclusively for them. Dale refused every offer. His motivation was simply to improve the quality of the meth he was consuming himself, and earn some cash on the side from teaching others who were similarly minded. As a keen fisherman, he dreamed of one day owning his own boat, of being able to fish in warm waters off the coast for big fish, but in the end, in December 2000, Dale's kidneys finally gave out and he died penniless.

Neta says that, for her family, her brother's legacy is bittersweet. 'He was a kind and gentle man,' she says. Yet everyone in the community knows what the newspaper said about Dale, the picture they painted of the wild, hillbilly satanist who was single-handedly cooking up a social epidemic in his Gympie kitchen. Sure, Dale changed the world of meth production forever but it seems more likely that he did that because his overactive mind saw meth production as a puzzle to be solved, not because he had a nefarious criminal plan. How his genius was transferred into dollars and cents was down to others.

Putting aside any judgement of whether drugs are 'bad' or not, I wonder if Neta feels any pride in Dale's achievement. His discovery was, after all, kind of a big deal.

'Our whole family is anti-drugs,' she says. Five days before his death, Neta visited Dale at home. She says he knew he was dying and was full of remorse. 'Dale apologised at the end, just before he died, for what he'd done.'

Despite his early demise, Dale's invention was going to have profound consequences outside of his control. The box lab was already being mass-produced and commercialised way beyond Queensland. His method crossed the Pacific when a meth producer in Colorado obtained his recipe from a criminal contact in Australia in 1996. The Colorado chemist then trained others and the hypo method spread rapidly to other states.

People everywhere were using his idea. Cooks who likely had no idea who Dale Francis Drake was were cooking meth his way. By 1997, hypophosphorous acid and iodine were being encountered by law enforcement at illicit laboratories in Oregon and California. The number of seizures in Colorado rose from 31 laboratories in 1998 to 455 laboratories in 2001—and they were predominantly using Dale's method.

The cops had been trumped. Dale had shown the way to the world's first DIY drug lab. The strategy of shutting down meth production by restricting the industrial supplies of red phosphorus had been circumvented by a talented amateur chemist who hadn't finished high school.

There was one solution staring everyone in the face. You could stop the box lab method dead by restricting the supply of ephedrine and pseudoephedrine itself. Without that key ingredient, it didn't matter what variations cooks like Dale came up with, they simply wouldn't have anything to work with. But there was one big obstacle to that policy: the pharmaceutical companies that were making billions from cold-and-flu remedies that contained ephedrine and pseudoephedrine weren't keen to give that up. Lobbying went on at the highest level to prevent any ban on drugs like Sudafed.

So Dale's box lab method endured until finally, eight years after his death, the Australian government came up with a compromise solution that sought to restrict the sale of over-the-counter cold remedies containing pseudoephedrine. The Poisons and Therapeutic Goods Regulation 2008 required pharmacists to ask for photo IDs of all customers buying products containing pseudoephedrine. Peter Vallely predicted at the time that the changes would remove what he called 'the Beavis and Butthead element—low-level drug cooks' and return production to the hands of organised criminals. If you couldn't get easy access to large quantities of 'pseudo', then Dale's hypo method wasn't worthwhile. Only the big boys who could find alternatives would stay in business. Unfortunately, time would prove Peter wrong.

―――――

The number of medium- and industrial-scale clandestine laboratories detected in Australia has remained relatively small. The reason for that is the proliferation of addict-based cooks running on much smaller quantities of pseudoephedrine. Kitchen cooks like Chris have popped up all over the country.

As I look around Chris's lean-to kitchen in Southport, with its corrugated-iron roof, lino flooring and old cabinets topped with porcelain tiles that look like they were made in the 1970s, I can still feel the spectre of Dale's ghost— Chris's setup is a far cry from a commercial meth lab. In the next room, a dog starts barking, a reminder that this is

Chris's home. He disappears momentarily and I can hear him yelling over the sound of a distant television for the dog to shut up.

Alone for a moment, I realise that I'm feeling very excited to be here. I've never seen or heard anyone describe the workings of even a small-scale meth-production process in detail before, and I've had to hustle hard to get inside one myself. Meth cooks aren't queuing up to share their secrets with the outside world. Maybe that is because getting caught operating a clan lab carries with it a lengthy prison sentence, or maybe it's because of the fear that your student might get it wrong. Ask any cook and they'll tell you that cooking meth isn't straightforward, and if you do get it wrong, the consequences could be severe—fatal, even. Cooking meth is a genuine 'Don't Try This At Home' activity.

To anyone foolish enough to read what I'm about to share and still be tempted to try it out, I'd say please ensure that you are alone; then, if you do blow yourself up, nobody else has to be a victim of your stupidity. Chris might be a meth addict but he is also a full-time cook who has performed the process a hundred times. Even knowing that, and watching him do it for the hundred-and-first time, I still feared for my safety every single second that I was locked inside his kitchen with him. There are many steps during a meth cook in which the whole thing can explode or catch fire. Trust me when I say that you'd have to be completely crazy to give this a go yourself.

I stand back, heart racing a little, back pressed against the locked door to get as far from the action as possible. I nod to Chris that I'm happy for him to start and, without fanfare, he begins to lay out what he needs, prepping his kit and ingredients on the benchtop the way a chef might get ready to cook a meal. Each time he touches something new he holds it up for me to see, starting with an ice compress, the kind that you'd see in most sports stores.

'They make most of 'em with urea these days,' he says, taking a pair of scissors and removing the crystals from inside the packet. 'So the AN [ammonium nitrate] ones are harder to find, but this brand works okay.'

With the ice-pack crystals carefully dissected, Chris shows me the other ingredients—a bottle of drain cleaner, a tin of camping-stove gas, a packet of Eveready batteries and a brand-new 2-litre plastic bottle.

'I like to use a new bottle, 'cos if there's any fluid in there, the whole thing can fucking blow,' Chris chuckles.

'Just to be clear,' I ask, 'this process is potentially explosive, isn't it?'

Chris considers his reply for a moment before he smiles ruefully. 'Nah, you'll be right, mate.'

Barely reassured, I watch as Chris takes a battery from the packet. Using an old pipe cutter, he carefully scores the battery around its middle and strips away the casing with a pair of pliers. He works quickly, his fingers nimble, and he doesn't even flinch when the battery gives off a little spark. I leap out of my skin. I can pick up the smell of rotten eggs in the room as he discards the casing, his fingers now black and inky from touching the dark guts inside.

'Lithium,' he says, as he unrolls the black lump like he's pulling apart a roll of film from the back of an old camera. It unfurls into a wide strip of dark foil around

15 centimetres long. This is the all-important ingredient, which catalyses the process.

'You gotta be careful to keep these dry,' he says, tearing the lithium into small pieces and dropping them into a ziplock bag containing a few generous splashes of camping fuel. 'Right, ready to go.'

I'm amazed. There's barely any equipment in the room that you'd associate with a school chemistry lab, let alone a meth lab. Other than the products I've mentioned, there are some crusty plastic bottles and grubby Tupperware, a bag of table salt and a hair dryer. I spot the detritus of previous 'cooks', including the telltale sign of empty boxes of Sudafed in a plastic bin on the floor.

Pseudoephedrine is still the magic ingredient in making meth. It may be harder to get hold of, but pseudoephedrine-based cold-and-flu remedies are still available on prescription from pharmacies, or where the purchaser is known or has been verified by photographic evidence. And where there's a will, there's a way. Chris says that users will bring him the 'good stuff'—Sudafed containing pseudoephedrine—as payment for his meth. One box in exchange for one point.

He picks up the plastic bottle and waves a hand over the rest of the mess. 'I can't show you the whole thing today,' he says. 'But if I get this one started, you'll see enough to get how it works. Follow what I do exactly and you won't go far wrong.'

Chris says that his lab probably contains around 200 bucks' worth of kit, most of which you can reuse.

'I probably need about fifty bucks' worth of new shit every time,' he estimates.

That's it. That's what it costs to get you up and running in the meth-production business on the Gold Coast. You could do it for less if you're happy to educate yourself. Most of the information about the method Chris uses is available to read online but he warns against that. Chris says it's better to get a demo in person to reduce your chances of 'stuffing up and causing a fire'.

Even these small laboratories represent a substantial health-and-safety threat to communities. The chemicals that Chris is using may be freely available but they are all toxic, highly flammable and/or corrosive. The production of 1 gram of meth releases toxic gases into the atmosphere and creates 5 or 6 grams of physical waste, which has to be disposed of somewhere. Fires and explosions are a constant threat.

Even though I've read about dozens of so-called 'shake-and-bake' meth labs exploding and burning to the ground, something about Chris's confidence leaves me feeling oddly reassured. He opens the top of the plastic bottle again, pours in the drain cleaner and ice-pack crystals, then adds the fuel containing the lithium and gives the mixture a gentle swirl.

'See that?' he asks, holding up the bottle so I can see that small bubbles have started to appear on the surface of the mixture.

He explains that the most important ratio in the process is the amount of lithium. Today, he's using a 24-gram box of Sudafed pills, which means he needs half a lithium battery strip. But he recommends adding an extra piece just to be safe. 'You can have too much lithium, but if you don't have enough, the result is unusable.'

He lets the contents of the bottle react and gives the bottle a gentle squeeze. 'Now we need to build the pressure up,' he says.

He takes the hair dryer and gives the mixture a quick blast of warm air. I can see the reaction begin to speed up inside the bottle. The crystals and the drain cleaner have started to turn the lithium a copper-brown colour, and more and more bubbles are escaping from the mixture. Chris's face is now creased up, concentrating hard, watching the pressure build inside the bottle, testing it constantly by squeezing it gently between finger and thumb. Finally, he licks his lips and sets the bottle down.

'Feel that!' he tells me. I hesitate to get closer to a potentially explosive event but I contain my fear enough to give the bottle a quick squeeze. It feels as though I'm squeezing a live hand grenade. It is solid, hard to the touch, like when you take a bottle of water up in an aeroplane.

'Yeah?' he says, checking that I'm paying attention. 'So, now we gotta let a bit of that pressure out.'

He carefully unscrews the cap, just a little, letting out a hiss of air that makes me jump. The room suddenly stinks of piss. 'Ammonia?' I ask.

Chris nods, with a smile. 'You know your stuff,' he quips.

For the next hour, Chris repeats the process of letting the pressure build up inside the bottle before releasing it again. Sometimes he gives it a little swirl to get it going again; sometimes he gives it another blast with the hair dryer. Watching him, I feel like he's a genuine craftsman at work, constantly keeping the reaction on a knife edge, agitating the chemicals until they are about to explode before he slows the whole thing down again. Over and over.

Sometimes when he unscrews the top, the ammonia rushes out with such a high-pitched hiss that I flinch, and again wonder if this is the point when things might blow. I keep thinking of a story I read about a Texan cook who had cooked meth hundreds of times until one day, a single droplet of sweat fell from his forehead into the bottle and it exploded right in his face, leaving him permanently scarred.

Eventually, everything inside the bottle settles down and Chris smiles. 'Okay, we're good.'

He vents the bottle one more time. I'm not entirely confident that the air I'm breathing isn't doing my lungs some damage, and I regret not putting on a mask before we started. It's probably too late now.

Chris takes a blender containing what he says are 'whizzed-up' Sudafed pills and tips the powder into the bottle before he tightens the lid. 'You need the high pressure at this stage if you want it to be good.'

He holds the bottle aloft. 'Now, you gotta shake the shit out of it.'

Chris shakes the plastic bottle that he's filled with camping-stove fluid and ice-pack salts, bits of batteries and powdered cold-and-flu pills, all sourced from local stores. He shakes and shakes it like a barman making a martini.

Every time he shakes, I see the mixture inside go viscous and dark brown like hot chocolate, and then, when he sets it down again, it settles into a clear solution. After a dozen or twenty shakes, Chris decides he's done enough.

He opens the top, releases the last bit of pressure and allows the mixture to settle for the final time. The liquid inside is clear, with a few brown lumps floating on the surface.

'Not bad,' he shrugs. I have no idea what he's measuring it against so I just grunt in agreement, breathing a sigh of relief that we seem to have passed the dangerous part of the process and our chances of being blown up have just reduced drastically.

Chris takes a clean funnel and packs it with cotton-wool balls and half a dozen coffee filters before he decants the mixture from the bottle, through the funnel into a clean Mason jar.

'Okay, now you got some choices,' Chris says. 'Some people will say you gotta wash it to get all the impurities out, but I say that's all bullshit.'

Chris means performing one more step that would remove the sulphur deposits that are left over from the chemical process. Some users have reported that without those impurities, the rush isn't as great when meth is injected. Others disagree. In any case, Chris is happy to proceed with what he has.

I'm transported back to my school chemistry lessons as I watch Chris use an eye-dropper to slowly add some hydrochloric acid drop by drop to the mixture in the jar, stirring and letting it settle before using another dropper to test the pH of the mixture in a swimming-pool testing kit. The acid gradually lowers the pH until it reaches a neutral 7, which Chris says is perfect for consumption.

We watch the mixture settle: the clear meth solution at the bottom, the leftover camping fuel floating at the top.

Using a syringe, Chris draws off the clear meth solution, squirting it onto a flat tray. As he dries it with the hair dryer, I can see the water evaporate until powdery white crystals appear on the tray.

'This is what I sell,' Chris says. 'If I can be fucked, I'll give it an acetone wash and recrystallise it in the fridge to get the big white crystals that people like. But it takes another few hours and it doesn't get you any more fucked than this shit does.'

Laid out on the tray in front of me is around 5 grams of methamphetamine. Created in a back-room meth lab before my very eyes, using products freely available in local stores. In less than two hours, Chris has turned fifty dollars' worth of everyday products into about four grand's worth of ice.

'Why not cook more?' I wonder. Chris explains that several factors make this method difficult to scale up—the challenge in obtaining Sudafed in bulk being the main one. Since the changes in legislation, cooks can't send stooges on Sudo-runs to hoover packs from the local pharmacy. The other limiter is safely controlling the chemical reactions to avoid explosions.

'Is that why you have the extinguisher?' I ask Chris, pointing to the dry chemical fire extinguisher in the corner.

'Always keep one of those handy, mate,' Chris says, without looking up. 'Seriously, you never know.'

I thank Chris for his tutorial and say goodbye, stepping back out into the street, walking past the tatty bungalows, wondering how many of them could have clandestine meth labs in their kitchens out back. As I was leaving, I had got the distinct feeling that Chris wasn't going to wait long before sampling his new batch. And that idea made me realise something important. Shake-and-bake labs may be ubiquitous—there may be 1000, 2000, 5000 Chrises out there—but these cooks are producing small quantities of meth at a time and shooting up most of it into their own veins.

Chris may be an important part of the story but he can't be the most important part. To understand what is, I need to know more about the makeup of Australia's meth supply. And to do that, I have to talk to someone who has access to detailed analysis of how it is being made—and, more importantly, where it might be coming from.

2

ANALYSE THIS

From a chemical point of view, the only difference between amphetamine (speed) and methamphetamine (meth) is that meth has one extra carbon and hydrogen molecule attached to it. You might not notice the difference if they're in powder or tablet form but you will easily spot meth if it is further purified into 'ice'—a smokable or injectable form of meth that consists of large, transparent, colourless, virtually pure crystals of methamphetamine hydrochloride.

As we saw in the previous chapter, many different chemicals can be used in the production of meth. These fall into three categories: precursors (the basic chemical 'building blocks'), reagents (chemicals that modify or combine precursors in a chemical reaction) and general-purpose chemicals (solvents, acids, alkalis and so on that facilitate the reaction and/or isolate the product).

In Australia, the sale of some precursors, reagents and chemicals is regulated by legislation, but the sale of many others is not. For the last twenty years, a game of cat and mouse has gone on between authorities and meth cooks as ingredients get banned and cooks come up with new ways to make meth. The cooks are ingenious and the authorities are engaged in a giant game of whack-a-mole.

There are now more than twenty known methods for producing meth but they nearly all use one of two precursors: either phenyl-2-propanone, an industrial chemical known as P2P, or ephedrine/pseudoephedrine, the main ingredient in cold-and-flu pills such as Sudafed. Ephedrine can also be extracted from ephedra plant products using common solvents but you need a lab to do that. So, for the most part, we're dealing with pseudoephedrine produced for snotty noses.

The choice of method used by cooks depends on various factors including the availability of precursors, the complexity of the process and the availability of equipment. Three main methods have emerged. Two use pseudoephedrine and the other one uses P2P.

The two 'pseudo' methods involve converting pseudo-ephedrine to methamphetamine using either an acid (hydriodic acid/red phosphorus—the *red phosphorus method*; or hypophosphorous acid/iodine—Dale Francis Drake's *'hypo method'*) or a reactive metal (lithium or sodium/ammonia—the 'Nazi method' used by Chris).

(Nobody is quite sure where the term 'Nazi method' came from. One story is that an enterprising young American cook found the recipe for it in an old science book in his local library in Oregon. The margin of the book was said to have been annotated with a swastika by a previous reader. But this story may be apocryphal.)

On the other hand, the P2P method has lots of variations but mainly involves producing methamphetamine using aluminium amalgam or formic acid (also known as the '*Leuckart method*').

If you were a fan of the TV show *Breaking Bad*, you might have spotted that in season one of the show, Jesse and Walter use pseudoephedrine and red phosphorus to make meth but then, as their ambitions grow, Walter comes up with a new pathway that uses a version of the P2P method. This is how he creates the 'blue meth' that becomes his signature. No chemist I've spoken with can explain why Walter's meth would have come out blue. Most likely it was added by the show's writers for dramatic effect.

The main drawback of the P2P method is that it produces two variations, or isomers, of methamphetamine—'d' and 'l'. The 'd' isomer is the one you want if you're using the drug recreationally as it creates the buzz. The 'l' variant is benign and offers none of those effects.

The advantage of the pseudo methods is that they only produce d-methamphetamine. But if you're using the P2P method, the l-isomer you produce has to be recycled via another complex chemical process, meaning that this method is more suited to big operations in which the cooks know what they're doing and the yields are high enough to warrant the additional processing. For that reason, P2P labs tend to knock out product in hundreds of grams, if not kilograms, at a time.

But which of these methods is most prevalent in the Australian supply chain?

The available data reveals a couple of clues. First, seizures of ephedrine and pseudoephedrine in Australia did not change significantly between 2015 and 2020, despite large increases in seizures of high-grade methamphetamine. This suggests that the current creeping market expansion is not related to meth cooked by the ephedrine/pseudoephedrine method, but rather the complex P2P methods favoured by bigger labs.

The emergence of the hypo method and, later, shake-and-bake methods have certainly democratised meth production to such an extent that now anyone can be a meth cook. Chris's lab is a great example of how, far from decreasing production, the new laws to control the flow of precursors have actually spread out small-scale meth production.

According to the latest report from the Australian Crime Intelligence Commission, the vast majority, somewhere around 80 per cent, of detected laboratories in Australia are addict-based or small-scale. At the same time, in the last twenty years, the proportion of discovered laboratories that are categorised as industrial-scale has fallen to less than 5 per cent.

That means that Chris's homemade lab now probably reflects the 'typical' Australian clandestine laboratory: addict-based, small-scale, residential location, using products and kit that are freely available within Australia, and without the need for specialist knowledge, sophisticated techniques or industrial chemicals.

But 10,000 Chrises couldn't produce enough meth to satisfy the national demand. The volume of meth that shake-and-bake cooks produce is simply not significant.

Looking forward, there's not much reason for shake-and-bake cooks to expand or decrease their overall market share either. Chris cooks up half a dozen grams at a time, which feeds his own habit with maybe a bit of surplus to sell. He's a self-sufficient enterprise. But that's it. It's not scalable beyond that, which is why shake-and-bake doesn't attract the big boys. For the criminal gangs, it's just not worth it.

The number of addict-based labs like Chris's therefore seems destined to remain fairly steady, and the volume of meth they produce pretty paltry. Meanwhile, the increasing demand must be being met elsewhere. It makes sense to conclude that the gangs behind the big labs are the ones picking up that extra demand in the market. Organised criminal groups have the resources to source the precursors, reagents and equipment that cooks like Chris could never do. With all the gear at their disposal, production runs can use the larger P2P method to churn out kilograms at a time.

Before we move on to look at where those labs might be, it's worth noting how police in Australia like to report in the media on the number of 'busted clan labs' they have uncovered, often blowing their own trumpets about how the numbers continue to rise year on year, as though that reflects great policing. But when the majority of these labs are small-time enterprises run by shake-and-bakers like Chris, busting them has little impact on the overall supply. The police should stop reporting on the number of lab seizures in their annual reports and focus instead on the volume of supply that has been interrupted. The main thing we're interested in is how much meth has been stopped from hitting the street, not how many small-time law-breakers they've charged with minor offences.

Arresting Chris is not the same as shutting down an industrial lab that produces 100 kilos of ice on each run. The real issue is how these detections impact the total supply on the street, but police seem reluctant to release that data—maybe because it wouldn't paint such a triumphant picture of their work.

Another factor we should consider is that bigger labs that knock out kilograms of meth tend also to produce meth at a much higher purity, which the market willingly absorbs. Another unfortunate consequence of policing that focuses on kitchen labs may be that it has led to an increase in the strength of meth on the streets.

Looking again at the data, we can see that purity back in the early 2000s was still low. Surveys done on quality rarely turned up street-level meth with purity over 30 or 40 per cent. Much of this meth was still termed 'speed' by users, and it looked more like a powder than a crystal. The truth was that users didn't really know the difference and probably didn't care much either. As long as the drug 'did the job', often you just had to accept that you got what you got. One day a user could be shooting kitchen-cooked low-grade powdered meth; the next day it might be higher-quality crystals produced in a super-lab.

And then, all of a sudden, the crystals that were turning up were of higher quality. In Victoria during the meth explosion of the 2000s, the police forensic services experts were routinely scanning purity levels in seizures and reported that there was one standout pattern starting to emerge: the purity levels of crystals were suddenly over

80 per cent. A user shooting crystal meth was getting a hit five or six times stronger than they were getting from powdered meth.

But where was the new high-grade crystal meth coming from? It wasn't (and still isn't) being produced in quantity by small cooks like Chris, or even by enterprising box lab cooks following Dale Francis Drake's method. All the cooks like Chris across Australia are together producing less than 1 per cent of the supply. So, either there were industrial-scale labs out in the bush somewhere knocking out ice by the tonne, or it was being imported from outside of the country. Which was it?

———

I put this question to Julian, the Queensland drug cop I spoke with in chapter one. He lists all the methods of producing methamphetamine that he has encountered during his career—ammonium methods, phosphorous methods, seven different pseudoephedrine methods, all perfectly capable of producing high-quality crystals. He confirms that the lithium methods, used in operations like Chris's, are now the favoured ones for small-scale methamphetamine producers but he says that the meth they produce is poor. You can spot it a mile away. The vast majority of meth on the streets is so much better than that now that he's confident it isn't coming from small-time home labs.

'Meth cooks are the most creative and adaptable people, and the smartest you're ever going to meet,' Julian says about his criminal adversaries. 'They find ways around everything. Sometimes you just go, "God, this is brilliant. Whoever came up with this is just brilliant."'

Which all makes Julian suspicious. He believes that the meth on the streets is coming from big labs, operated by top chemists and people with real chemical intelligence, but where they're located is a mystery.

'We're not finding those labs anymore,' he says. 'We know that supply levels are up. We know from the purity levels that they're not coming from shake-and-bake labs. So where are they coming from?'

There are some clues. First, there was a marked increase in detections of ice at the Australian border after 2000. Large-scale ice importations came in with sea freight originating from South-East Asia. These looked remarkably similar in their origin and nature to the large-scale heroin shipments that the Australian Federal Police (AFP) had worked hard to stop.

The first significant seizure was 79 kilos of ice in November 2000. After that, the quantities steadily increased until May 2003, when 233 kilos of ice was detected in a shipping container carrying rice sticks from China. This seemed to be proof that a significant proportion of the new high-purity meth in crystal form that was turning up on the streets of Sydney and Melbourne was coming from China.

Does that mean that the new high-quality ice available in Australia was all imported? It's certainly a reasonable assumption, given that ice started to appear on Australian streets at the same time that large-scale shipments of ice were first detected at the Australian border. It's also consistent with the fact that in the early 2000s, very few of the clandestine laboratories busted by the cops were producing crystalline product on any scale. Only true enthusiasts and skilled chemists were bothering to refine their speed into ice.

So, for me, the question remains: where are the super-labs that are knocking out hundreds of kilograms of high-quality ice now? Are they in Australia? Are they in China? Who is running them? And how do they operate? Big lab busts in Australia still make big headlines but they are rare.

Andrew Parkinson is Coordinator Crime Scenes with the Australian Federal Police. Andrew's very senior role includes overseeing the forensic response to AFP investigations within Australia and internationally. He explains to me that every time the AFP seize a quantity of meth, whether it be at a border seizure, a drug bust or a clandestine lab raid, samples of the drugs are sent to their forensic team for chemical analysis. From the impurities left behind in the cooking process, his team are able to see exactly what precursor chemicals were used to make the drugs, and even what process was employed. Different drug-producing regions of the world leave their own telltale clues in the meth they produce, allowing their product to be identified.

What he's spotted in the samples echoes what Julian told me: production from Australian super-labs has dropped off and, as a result, seizures here are getting rarer.

'Our state and territory police just aren't seizing the same ice they once did,' Andrew says. 'We do see still some product from big labs in Australia, but they're dwarfed by the amount of importations. Our importations have gone through the roof.'

Andrew says the vast majority of samples he sees now indicate that they're coming from major importers as opposed to local manufacturers, but he says that the purer the meth gets, the harder the identification process becomes.

'We can usually tell the source from the impurities, but a lot of the methamphetamine that's come out of Asia is really high purity—close to one hundred per cent methamphetamine. So that limits some of our ability to determine exactly what reagents have been used in the conversion.'

Andrew says that users on the street are able to spot these as well, although they're using firsthand experience rather than sophisticated chemical analysis. And they seem to be enjoying the new supply.

'There's a real thirst for South-East Asian–manufactured methamphetamine in the Australian market,' Andrew says.

I wonder if the AFP have formed a view about how the Asian cooks are manufacturing meth. Are they reducing pseudoephedrine or using the P2P method?

'Traditionally we were dominated by pseudoephedrine-produced methamphetamine, a lot of it coming from China,' he says. 'But we've seen a dramatic increase in P2P meth in the last couple of years, to the point where it's now maybe fifty-fifty.'

According to official figures provided to me by the AFP, the total weight of forensically tested methamphetamine in 2021 was 2752 kilograms. Analysis revealed that more than 2300 kilograms of that—about 84 per cent—was produced from P2P. Andrew's comment about the dramatic increase was right; the year before, in 2020,

P2P had accounted for just over 41 per cent of all the meth analysed by the AFP. Now that estimate seems low. The trend is clear—large-scale producers in the market are not using pseudoephedrine anymore. The production has shifted to a method more suited to industrial-scale production.

With the permission of the AFP, I spoke anonymously with another three agents who cover the South-East Asian region, working in the field. They asked for their identities to be concealed so that they could talk more freely. Each of them has firsthand experience of intercepting shipments of methamphetamine coming into Australia. I wondered which ports were being particularly targeted.

According to the agents, Sydney and Melbourne have been taking it in turns to be the port of choice for some time, probably because the sheer volume of their traffic gives the smugglers more cover. In 2021–22, there were over a dozen seizures at these two ports that ran into the hundreds of kilograms. In three out of the last four meth-amphetamine busts, the drugs were concealed inside heavy machinery sent from Malaysia.

'Keep an eye on the news, though,' the voice on the line tells me, 'because we're about to release pictures of the most recent, one of our largest ever seizures in fact, off the coast of Perth. I think that'll come out in the next week or two.'

The Perth seizure occurred on a fishing vessel, which had loaded up from a ship that originated in Yangon port in Myanmar. The agents believe a so-called 'mothership' was loaded with methamphetamine very close to the Myanmar coast and covered the ocean until it unloaded onto the smaller vessel bound for the Western Australian port.

How do the AFP find these shipments? Thousands of ships, boats and aeroplanes land in Australia every week. 'It's very intelligence led,' the agent replies. 'The Thais do some good work with human sources, especially up to the north. So we do some good joint operations with them.'

Most of the drugs found in Perth were packed inside Chinese green-tea packets; the green-tea packet is a sign of quality, an underground brand that signifies where the drugs originated. The shipment's intended buyers, mostly outlawed motorcycle gangs in Australia, covet the green-tea methamphetamine above all else.

Hearing this triggers a memory and as soon as I'm off the phone, I'm scrolling through old photos until I find the one that my producer friend sent to me when I was in LA years before. Sure enough, lying next to the dead criminal informant shot by the Thai DEA are piles of methamphetamine packaged in green-tea packets.

The AFP agents share with me their latest intelligence. The biggest shipments coming into Australia over the last couple of years have been predominantly arriving by sea. Black flights, so-called because the planes are small and fly too low to be detected by radar, are incredibly rare. One of the agents explains that these planes can't carry the required volume of cargo to make the risk worthwhile. Industrial shipments and larger commercial fishing vessels are the preferred modes of transport.

By any measure, you'd have to say that the AFP have been very successful at intercepting these shipments. Close to half of all the meth coming into Australia is intercepted, which in 2020 meant that 8 tonnes was stopped at the border. That's impressive . . . but what happened to the other 11 tonnes that wasn't intercepted?

That's where Australia's organised criminal groups take over the story. Bikie groups, in particular the Comancheros and Hells Angels, have been particularly dominant in the distribution of meth within Australia. Both have achieved their success, the agents tell me, by fostering strong ties with meth-producing gangs in Asia.

It certainly makes sense that these groups would move away from cooking meth themselves within Australia. Why risk importing the chemicals you need to cook meth yourself if there are networks in Asia, and factories that will distribute those chemicals to clandestine labs elsewhere in the region, run by gangs who sell it to you at knockdown prices with delivery guarantees?

Andrew Parkinson says that the AFP have recently identified factories in southern China that are producing the precursor chemicals necessary for production. Whoever is buying those chemicals is supplying the labs with everything they need to produce the best-quality meth he's ever seen. There's still a lack of conclusive evidence where exactly those labs are located because nobody has been able to access them to see for themselves. If they did, they might have the smoking gun that proves that the majority of Australia's meth is coming from somewhere in South-East Asia.

Talking to Andrew and the other AFP agents, I already know that the answer to that question lies abroad. The overwhelming majority of meth on the streets of Australia in 2023 is being produced industrially using P2P, then imported through the ports of Sydney, Melbourne and Perth. I'm sure now that the source of that meth is not the kitchens of Southport but the jungles of Asia. But where exactly is still uncertain.

It's clear to me that if I want to find out more about that supply then I have to meet some bigger operators—people who are cooking kilograms, not grams. I have to find the people who operate at the top end of the supply chain. To do that, I need to look further afield.

3

THE ASIAN CONNECTION

Every week, the Australian press contains reports of meth busts up and down the country. Vast quantities of the drug keep turning up in police seizures from Perth to Brisbane, Adelaide to Sydney. One raid in Melbourne intercepted a shipment of more than 1.5 tonnes. Yes, you read that correctly—*tonnes*. In a Channel 7 News item on the seizure, the street value was reported to be over A$1 billion. I'll say more about reported street values later but even though this number is a gross exaggeration, we're still talking about a significant find. What is undeniably accurate in the report is that the drugs were hidden inside stereo speakers sent from Bangkok.

The Channel 7 report stopped short of speculating on how the drugs got as far as the port in Bangkok. This is the case for most media packages about smuggled drugs.

The port from which the drugs leave Asia is more often than not the final place that gets a mention. Sometimes a story might go so far as to suggest that the producers were 'Asian drug gangs' or that the route stemmed from somewhere 'in rural Thailand', but rarely do they investigate further than that. There seems to be a general lack of curiosity about who is actually behind the trade. It's for that reason that I've decided to fly to Bangkok. I want to try to find out more about where these shipments originate within Asia.

My hunch is that the Meth Road is not a single track but a complex network of interconnected highways, with off-ramps and bridges, tunnels and roundabouts that enable many branch roads to feed traffic efficiently from all corners of the region. Unless we get a grip on exactly how that network operates, we'll never fully understand where the supply of drugs is coming from. And if we don't know that, then I feel efforts to disrupt the supply side of the market will remain ineffective.

It seems to me that there are several components we need to understand about the Asian end of the Meth Road. Working backwards, it stands to reason that the shipments entering Australia's ports must be finding their way onto the open seas from Asian ports, which begs the question, 'How?'

The criminals must have networks capable of delivering the drug from the inland production facilities to the ports on the shore. The land routes they have developed must be capable of avoiding whatever national law enforcement efforts are in place to apprehend them. I want to understand how these channels are fuelled at their source, who is behind the production, and how they can keep knocking out tonnes and tonnes of meth without detection.

––––––

The United Nations Office on Drugs and Crime (UNODC) seems a good place to start. They produce countless reports on the Asian drug economy and have done for more than twenty years.

The UNODC employs nearly 2000 people across the world and has a budget upwards of US$700 million per year. It's been around since the mid-1990s and its stated aim is to provide research, guidance and support to member states that are at the sharp end of the 'war on drugs', helping them to battle not only the trafficking and abuse of drugs but the criminal activities associated with it, from money laundering to piracy.

Today, the South-East Asian regional office of the UNODC operates out of a sprawling, low-rise, bright-green building shaped like a lizard's tail in the centre of Bangkok. It's 35 degrees outside so when I step inside, I'm grateful for a refreshing blast of cool from the air conditioning. The receptionist invites me to take a seat, so I sit and watch suited diplomats come and go while I wait to be called.

The UNODC's Bangkok office has become the epicentre for the collection and analysis of all intelligence on the Asian meth trade. The people passing by are the ones tasked with monitoring the drug trade, the people who every year produce all the reports and surveys that intricately detail the size and nature of the industry. I can't help but wonder if any of them have ever stepped far from their air-conditioned offices into the field.

What the UNODC do have access to is state-of-the-art laboratories. Their most recent report reached similar conclusions to the AFP—that the nature and quality of methamphetamine hitting the streets of Australia has changed markedly over recent years. According to the report, the ice that is being apprehended at Asia's ports is close to 100 per cent purity. The report goes on to argue that with such access to unlimited pure ice, there is no longer any incentive for gangs in Australia to produce ice themselves. The UNODC is arguing, much like the AFP, that all or nearly all of the ice on the streets of Australia now is imported directly from South-East Asia.

The UNODC argument goes that the Australian gangs have calculated that importing the final product is less risky for two reasons. First, the peak risk of getting caught during production occurs at the point of cooking, when you're making a telltale noxious smell that could give you away. Not needing your own lab takes away the risk of detection. Secondly, 10 kilograms of precursor (e.g. pseudo-ephedrine) is needed to make 1 kilogram of the final product. So importing the final product effectively reduces your material by 90 per cent, which in turn reduces your chances of getting caught by customs by 90 per cent too. The UNODC believe that it was a no-brainer for the gangs to outsource production.

It's certainly compelling logic, although I have two issues—or one issue and one question. My issue is that there's another consideration at play for someone deciding whether to cook or import 100 kilos of meth: what's the penalty if I get caught at the border? One hundred kilos of meth will land me in jail for twenty years, but even if I need ten times as much pseudoephedrine to make 100 kilos of meth, getting caught with a tonne of pseudo will carry a much lighter sentence. That's a pretty strong incentive to cook, albeit that I now have the additional risk of getting caught while I'm cooking.

The question I have is: why turn to Asia? Why not, say, Africa or Central America?

I believe the answer is twofold. First, the unique property of meth as a recreational drug is its ability to be manufactured from synthetic chemicals. Unlike cocaine or heroin, there's no plant to grow; there's nothing location-specific about meth production other than access to synthetic chemicals that are ubiquitous in Asia's factories.

Ever since a Japanese chemist, Nagai Nagayoshi synthesised methamphetamine in the 1890s, enterprising cooks have found new pathways to production. As far back as World War II, meth was being produced and marketed in Japan as *hiropon*, the Japanese pronunciation of the brand name Philopon, a portmanteau of the Greek words for 'love' and 'work'. *Hiropon* was allegedly given to Japanese soldiers to increase alertness, and to kamikaze pilots to suppress their fear of death. Later Taiwanese cooks developed new, inventive methods of meth production, exporting their techniques to covet laboratories in China and the Philippines where access to industrial chemicals was easy and cheap. Today, cooks from Taiwan are still regarded as the best in the world.

This is a very Asian narrative. Even though chemists around the world have since copied recipes from one another, I believe that, fundamentally, meth began as an Asian drug whose legacy has endured.

The other answer to the question 'Why Asia?' almost certainly lies in Australia's international trade figures. Six out of Australia's ten largest trading partners are in Asia. None are in Latin America. Legitimate trade routes are the means by which businesses open up shipping lanes and flight paths, but without a kosher trade to piggyback on, the drug smugglers have no way to move their drugs. While the EU and US have considerable legitimate trade connections with cocaine-producing regions of the world, Australia does not. The result is that the Mexican cartel is at a competitive disadvantage when it comes to Australia, leaving their Asian rivals to seize the opportunity to export an alternative stimulant that rivals cocaine.

Some signs are emerging that the Mexican cartel is trying hard to muscle in on a slice of the Australian market, but for now its influence is still relatively small compared to Asia. Asia is and has for many years been responsible for almost all of the seizures of meth headed for Australia. In 2010 there were fewer than 10 tonnes of meth seized in East and South-East Asia; by 2020 that number had increased to more than 79 tonnes.

But Asia is a big place. Where in Asia is the meth coming from is the question that I've come here to answer. The last UNODC audit of embarkation points for methamphetamine trafficked to Australia done in 2017 found that there's been a shift. Before 2015, the top spots for meth smuggling were China and Hong Kong but almost overnight, Thailand and Malaysia took over. So what changed? Why did China go from being the number one producer of Australian meth to an also-ran?

Back in the UNODC office in Bangkok, a young Thai man in a suit invites me to follow him through security. We pass along endless corridors to the office of the UNODC's Regional Representative for Southeast Asia and the Pacific, Jeremy Douglas.

Jeremy looks like your standard career diplomat: mid-forties, clean-cut, well-heeled and effortlessly confident. He sips a latte as he rattles off a boatload of statistics and references to various reports that he has overseen during his time as regional director. Jeremy says that the gangs behind the meth labs in China have upped sticks and moved production beyond China's borders.

He hands me a report that details how between 2014 and 2017, the Chinese government, waking up to the damage illegal meth production was doing to their international reputation, took action to divert supplies. This seems at odds with high-profile media reports that have been outing China as the primary source of Australia's meth. As recently as 2017, a major piece by *Time* magazine claimed that 'China has the largest number of clandestine ice labs in the Asia-Pacific region and is the source of most [of the ice] in Australia'.

But Jeremy says that to claim that in 2017 was already woefully out of date. By then, the Chinese Communist Party had already decided to remove the stain on their reputation caused by meth labs. Over the years, I have found that China and its inner workings can be a frustratingly opaque area of research but Jeremy says there is compelling evidence that the authorities there did conduct a 'cleanup' operation that took out some incredibly large, industrial-sized meth labs in southern China's Fujian and Guangdong regions.

But as China cleaned up its act, more recent research turned up something very odd. As Fujian and Guangdong were dismantling their meth labs and shunting the people behind them elsewhere, the number of labs getting raided in other parts of Asia started to drop. In 2015, 526 laboratories were dismantled across the region, but in the year to October 2018, only 130 laboratories were uncovered. Jeremy says that number has continued to fall year on year.

Is that an indication that production is slowing down?

'Quite the opposite,' he says. 'Supply has actually increased.'

The data backs him up. Certainly, the Chinese raids haven't impacted significantly on the quantities of meth turning up in Australia. The reason, Jeremy believes, is that almost all of the meth supplied to the Australian market now comes from one country that five years ago wasn't even on the UNODC's radar.

'The gangs have moved the labs out of the firing line in China and set up in places where it is safer to operate,' Jeremy says. 'Everything going into Australia now comes from Myanmar—and it's purer. Myanmar is now producing the best meth in the world.'

That last assertion, he explains, comes from that all-important chemical analysis that the UN conducts on Asian drug seizures. Just like the AFP, when the drug enforcement agencies of Thailand or Malaysia uncover a shipment of meth bound for Oz, they send samples to the UNODC labs for analysis. What they've been discovering is that the quality is on the up. When looked at alongside the fact that the quantities of meth being seized are also on the rise, it points to one very disturbing scenario: that the meth industry has relocated and is maturing very well.

But why does the UN think it's coming from Myanmar? Why not, say, Laos or Vietnam?

Jeremy shows me a news story from March 2019. Malaysian authorities reported the seizure of more than 2 tonnes of ice in the state of Johor, the largest amount ever seized in the country. He says their intel suggests that the drugs originated from Myanmar. The same month, a Myanmar naval ship intercepted a fishing boat off the southern tip of Myanmar carrying 1737 kilograms of ice presumed to be headed for one of the larger ports in Thailand. I'm reminded too of the AFP agents who told me about their latest seizure: a shipment caught off the coast of Western Australia, originating from Myanmar.

It seems that a network has developed whereby meth produced in Myanmar is being exported internationally using Malaysia and Thailand as stopovers on the route to Australian markets. Of course that requires the producers in Myanmar to use a network of regional smugglers to get the drugs out of the country. Which begs the question—*how?*

If these recent seizures are anything to go by, then at least some of the meth leaving Myanmar must be doing so by sea. Myanmar shares a coastline with Thailand and Malaysia, and the largest port serving it is in the country's largest city, Yangon. It seems the obvious place to continue my investigation so the next day I book a seat on one of a dozen flights leaving Bangkok for Yangon, the city once known as Rangoon, back when Myanmar was still called Burma.

———

When British troops invaded the former Burmese capital, Mandalay, in 1885, the Burmese king was exiled, Burma was officially annexed, and the process of dominating a foreign country both culturally and commercially began in earnest.

The British brought missionaries to found schools all over the country so that Christianity and English could be taught to Burmese children. The strategy destroyed the influence of Buddhist monks, who until then had been the primary educators of young Burmese men.

Meanwhile, the colonialists began exploiting Burma's vast teak forests in the south, simultaneously expanding rice production on the land. Vast numbers of people migrated across the country to work, clearing the way for more rice. Rangoon (now Yangon) was declared the new capital and the port expanded to feed the growing export markets in Europe.

When the British turned their attention to the eastern areas of Shan and Kachin states, they decided that they were too remote, too dangerous and too malaria-ridden to be bothered with. So, in exchange for some formal acceptance of central government authority and payment of taxes, the British granted individual chiefs areas of autonomy.

Until then, all Burmese had been treated equally, irrespective of ethnicity, ruled by a single monarch under one uniting faith. Now, under the British, they were a people divided. It was a classic British strategy of divide and rule that they successfully exploited all over their empire.

But when the British withdrew abruptly during World War II, Burma was left in ruins. The retreating British destroyed the infrastructure to ensure that none of the country's ports, mines, factories, refineries or rice lands fell into the hands of their Japanese enemies.

As soon as the war ended, the ethnic groups in Burma—divided, skint and angry—turned on each other and funded their battles by growing the only cash crop they knew: opium. The next fifty years saw the country become the world's largest producer of opium poppy, exporting heroin to fund an endless civil war.

The British Empire had inadvertently created the world's first narco-state.

———————

'I'm Banyar Aung,' says the man to my right as he slides his business card across the fine white tablecloth towards me. 'Nice to meet you.'

Last night I flew north from Bangkok to Yangon. Almost as soon as I landed, an old friend living here invited me to a black-tie dinner at the Yangon Pegu Club, a 150-year-old building, originally built as a hangout for British gentlemen stationed here during the days of colonial occupation. The grand, vaulted, teak ceiling of the Pegu's Great Hall is quite the location—wall-to-wall colonial grandeur, packed with the great and good (and rich) of Yangon's new social elite.

While war rages around the rest of Myanmar, Yangon, the economic capital of the country, is relatively stable. At the time of writing in 2023, Myanmar was experiencing heavy fighting in the north, south and east of the country, but the generals who seized control in a coup d'état after Aung San Suu Kyi won a majority in the 2020 election have established security in Yangon.

The host for this evening's festivities, Deborah Kyaw Thaung, a wealthy Burmese heiress and socialite who has been responsible for the Pegu Club's restoration, stands and formally welcomes her guests with a toast. Banyar leans over and whispers to me that she's his sister-in-law.

'This room was originally built for King Edward VII in celebration of his marriage and anticipation of his visit to Yangon with his new bride,' Deborah reads from her cue cards. 'Although they never actually turned up.'

A polite titter ripples through the hall as I turn over Banyar's card and cast my eyes over it. I look again at the man sitting next to me, suddenly a lot more interested in him than in the history of the Pegu Club. According to his card, the small, well-groomed man in black-tie and shiny shoes sitting next to me is the head of TMT, one of Yangon's five international shipping ports.

'Could I come and see you tomorrow?' I ask. 'I'd love to see inside the port.'

Since I met with the UNODC in Bangkok, one thing has been bothering me—if Myanmar is producing so much ice that Australia is receiving shipments by the tonne, then how exactly are the drugs making their way out of Myanmar? Australia is 8000 kilometres away by sea. There's only one way a would-be drug smuggler could move a tonne of ice that distance and that's on a ship. It occurs to me that Banyar might be the guy to help me work out how.

The next morning, nursing a minor hangover from one Pegu Club cocktail too many, I take a walk down to the port. I pass a noisy and expensive-looking primary school as the school run is in full swing. The street is packed with expensive four-wheel drives, and parents stand at the gates, waving off their little darlings. Most of the houses in this part of town are large and fancy. It's a curious fact that property in Yangon costs more per square metre than in London, New York or Sydney. Why would that be? Where could all the money be coming from?

I turn down a road that runs to the Yangon River and everything changes. Downtown Yangon is a different world, noisy and smelly, with open sewers running alongside cracked and broken pavements. There's a stall selling fresh noodles on every corner, customers perched on child-sized stools at knee-high tables, scoffing their breakfast. Unlike Bangkok, or the Lao capital, Vientiane, there are no motorbikes in Yangon city. The military junta have banned them out of a senior general's distaste for two-wheeled transport.

The absence of mobile phones in Yangon is shockingly apparent too. There seems something almost old-fashioned about people looking up at you as they walk along the street. The women of Myanmar like to decorate their faces with Thanaka, a yellow, ground-up tree bark which they smear over their cheeks—partly for protection from the sun, partly decorative. It adds to the sense that I am stuck somewhere in time, of people living in the past, ignorant of the technological revolution that has stimulated so much cultural change throughout the rest of Asia.

When I arrive at the entrance to TMT, a huge commercial shipping port along the bank of the river, a security guard leads me inside the belly of the port to the door of an office, where I'm met again by the warm and welcoming smile of the congenial Banyar Aung.

Banyar looks more relaxed in his workwear. He's a jolly-faced, rotund man with round spectacles that sit awkwardly on the end of his nose and look incongruous with his yellow hard hat. He speaks English beautifully, in a high, gentle register that suggests an education that didn't come for free. When I shake his hand, I notice that it is delicate and smooth, not the callused hand of a stevedore. I'm guessing that Banyar didn't work his way up to the top job.

Banyar takes me on a tour of the port, explaining how the operation is one of five shipping hubs in Yangon that transport goods to and from destinations all over the world. The Yangon River runs into the heart of the city, allowing trucks, loaded with containers, to drop off everything—from rice and coffee to timber—to huge ships that pull up along the dock. In peak season a port like TMT deals with more than 3000 containers in a week.

I ask him how he has been affected by the recent meth busts that Jeremy told me about in Bangkok. He immediately sighs deeply.

'When one of the ports gets busted and drugs are found,' he says, shaking his head, 'it's the port boss who takes the blame but actually that's the job of customs.'

Banyar explains how he works for his clients, the suppliers and hauliers, but working alongside the Myanmar customs authorities is part of the job. Ultimately though, even though he is not responsible for checking what goes in and out of the country, Banyar has a unique perspective on what's going on.

Who gets stopped by customs is based on a range of factors. Some things always get checked—sugar, for example, because it's easy to hide things in a container of sugar. Other things are picked up at random or because the supplier is considered high risk.

'Thirty-five to forty per cent of containers are considered high risk and have to be opened up,' says Banyar. 'Another thirty to thirty-five per cent get scanned with the X-ray machines. And all the sugar and rice get scanned every time.'

It sounds like a very thorough operation. Factors such as the route or the timing of the arrival of the truck can lead to closer inspection too. Late arrivals, containers coming in the middle of the night or at the last minute before the ship leaves are considered high risk and always get checked. It's impossible to fake the documentation and anyone who is caught can't get away. The port has all the driver's details, all the agent's details and all the links needed to make arrests.

But despite all those safeguards, the evidence is clear that busts are still being made in connection to Myanmar. In May 2018, Malaysian authorities at Port Klang, about 40 kilometres south-west of Kuala Lumpur, seized a 1.2-tonne shipment of ice as it was being transferred into the Malay port from a smaller container ship originating from Yangon. The larger ship was bound for Australia and the ice was disguised in green-tea packets.

But why stop in Malaysia at all? Why not just ship the drugs directly from Myanmar to Oz?

'No ships are going direct between Myanmar and Australia,' Banyar explains. 'They have to stop to reload in Thailand or Malaysia or Singapore.'

So how did the smugglers even get the drugs that far? How could they have bypassed the rigorous customs procedures in Yangon?

'You can't do it alone,' he says. 'Your network has to be very good because of all the people involved. You need an inside man in customs, the port authority, even on the vessels, the boat operators . . . You need a very big network.'

I'm curious how Banyar would approach the challenge of smuggling a tonne of ice out of Myanmar if he were a smuggler. Ask a logistics expert a logistics question and you'll get a logical answer. As soon as he hears my question, Banyar's eyes light up. He bounces out of his seat and walks over to the huge map of Myanmar that's hanging on the wall. I can see the cogs of his brain whirring as he considers the possibilities.

With his little finger, Banyan traces a line down the Yangon River until he reaches a point around 30 kilometres from the port. This is the spot where ships coming into Myanmar have to wait for a pilot to guide them safely into port. Banyar says the big ships can wait hours or even days in the river while they wait for a pilot to come aboard. That's the perfect time for smaller boats to sneak around the blind side of the bigger ship, loading contraband where nobody can see. But Banyar says he still thinks it's an incredibly difficult thing to pull off.

'You need a lot of luck because with all the checks, customs still have a 70 per cent chance of catching you.'

Seventy per cent sounds pretty risky. Banyar nods.

'Too risky,' he says. 'If I want to take a tonne of ice to Australia then I won't bring it through Yangon at all.'

He turns back to the map, but now his focus is on the other side of the country. He slides his finger along the Thailand–Myanmar border in the east. He stops and circles one particular area towards the south of the country that borders Thailand.

'I would go through here,' he says, pointing to the area. 'Carry it over the border in smaller packs and then, when you get to Thailand, you can move it onto the water using small domestic boats. Thailand has four or five times the capacity as us. Much easier to hide.'

He looks happy with this plan. Like he's cracked it. Just get it to Thailand and the job becomes considerably more feasible. Problem is, I suspect carrying a tonne of drugs over the Thai border is a lot easier said than done.

'Yes,' Banyar agrees. 'Still risky but much less than passing through Yangon.'

———

Standing high on a hill in northern Thailand, on the Myanmar border, I can see across a lush green valley that separates the two countries less than 700 metres away. All around me, the hill is protected by a line of military barricades topped with razor wire. Every 50 metres, along the ridge, there is a sentry point manned by two Thai soldiers whose guns are trained on the opposite side of the valley and close by is a small village of no more than fifty houses. Next to me, Colonel Sutkhet points into the distance and I follow his finger as he traces a line along the Ruak River, which forms the border between Thailand and Myanmar.

'The drugs come in from there, Wan Nam Lok—Ban Long,' he says pointing at the village in the distance. 'Over the river and normally this way, or they come through here.'

The colonel points to two spots along the valley where he says his men have encountered smugglers bringing meth into Thailand. Often he says the smugglers will arrive on foot, carrying the meth in backpacks, just as Banyar had described in Yangon. Once in Thailand, they quickly transfer their cargo into vehicles and drive to the ports on the other side of the country.

The colonel leads a division of the Phamuang, a Thai military anti-drugs task force that works side by side with the Thai DEA. Last month he says the Phamuang encountered a driver who accelerated towards their checkpoint. The colonel's men opened fire at the car, which skidded off the road. Somehow, the driver survived the crash and escaped into the jungle. The following day, the colonel appeared in the local paper, proudly standing in front of several kilos of ice and thousands of meth pills that his men discovered in the boot of the car.

'When the driver saw the checkpoint, he panicked, so my men opened fire,' he tells me. 'We hit the vehicle six times.'

Every week, it seems there's a similar news story from these northern Thai border areas. In 2021, the combined forces of the Phamuang and the Thai DEA confiscated more than 22 tonnes of crystal methamphetamine. That was up from 8 tonnes in 2017.

It strikes me, looking along the vast jungles that span the river, that there are too many points where the smugglers can cross for the Thai forces to effectively control it all. Especially when the colonel says that the new method favoured by the smuggling gangs is to bring the drugs over the river during the night. The Ruak River is hundreds of kilometres long and often only a few metres wide. To try to block any one path would be futile.

The colonel says that last month's bust relied on intel received from a criminal informant. To ensure that the intel they gather is accurate, he says that the Phamuang works with a wide network of CIs. With more than 2000 kilometres of border to police, without the intel, you'd have no chance. Even if you knew drugs were coming through the border at a specific time, you'd still have no idea where or how or when. Last month's seizure only happened because the CI source shared where and when exactly the car would be coming from the river area.

Did you arrest the driver?

'No. He fled.'

The colonel explains that it was so dark that when the driver ran into the deep forest, he was too fast for them. And the rules in Thailand say that you cannot shoot from behind. I must look surprised because he continues.

'We have to be safe. We don't know if he has guns or other weapons.'

But you're the army, I say.

'We're a little bit disappointed,' he concedes, 'but we got the drugs, so it's okay.'

On another recent bust, the Phamuang received intel from a CI that the village across the river from where we are standing was being used to store a significant quantity of drugs. For two days the colonel's men waited but saw nothing. Then, on the third day, the smugglers arrived around 7 p.m. Twenty men, four armed with AK-47s, the others carrying backpacks, each loaded with 20 kilos of ice, emerged from the forest. When the colonel's men shouted at them to stop, the smugglers opened fire.

'When they opened fire, they shot at us, they were ready to fight. They were ready to kill us and ready to die.'

Nothing is scarier than someone ready to die. How many arrests were made, I wonder?

The colonel gives me a sideways glance. Again, nobody was arrested.

This is a common outcome of reported seizures along the border. The narrative is nearly always that the drugs are discovered on a tip-off and no arrests are made, or that a vehicle or group on foot is identified and a gunfight ensues, after which the traffickers are either shot dead or they escape into the forest. Rarely is anyone arrested. Looking at media reports for significant seizures made by the Phamuang in 2019, the pattern is clear.

28 December 2019: 600 kilograms ice—13 escaped—2 deceased
17 December 2019: 4.9 million pills—all escaped
16 December 2019: 1.5 million pills—all escaped
6 October 2019: 40 kilograms ice—all escaped

11 August 2019: 4.1 million pills—no arrests
27 June 2019: 5 million pills, 185 kilograms ice—no arrests
12 May 2019: 340 kilograms ice—26 escaped—4 deceased

Not a single arrest.

The colonel says that the big suppliers on the other side of the border are making meth in all forms: meth pills for the Thai market and ice for the international market. In many cases, when the ice and pills come from different suppliers, they team up and use the same smuggling networks. You can't understand the ice trade without understanding the trade in meth pills too.

Meth pills, known in Thailand as yaba (which translates as 'crazy medicine'), have been the most common form of meth seen in South-East Asia since the 1990s. Yaba is made by blending low-grade methamphetamine and caffeine powder with a bonding agent and a dye. The mixture is put through a pill press and marked with a trademarking stamp. WY pills are the market leader and the UNODC estimates that billions of yaba pills pour across the Myanmar border every year.

The colonel says that his men apprehended a smuggler only last week as he was crossing the river with a backpack full of tea packets. When they searched the bag, they found that each packet contained 20,000 yaba pills, vacuum-sealed to keep them dry. Some of the packages were marked with a '999' stamp; others were emblazoned with 'Y1', denoting a different supplier. A bust of this size is so common that it didn't even make the local news.

I wonder what the colonel would do if he had all the resources he could dream of. He says that top of his list would be to invest in improving their intel system.

'We have to hire more CIs,' he says, 'so more money to expand that system would be top of my list. Because even a hundred checkpoints without intel won't work.'

Would undercover operations on the other side of the border be useful?

'That would be good,' he nods. 'If there was a budget to use CIs to work undercover over there that would be great.'

For now, he says that his team must groom CIs for themselves. Yesterday, his men caught a teenager with 1000 yaba tablets at the border. A haul of that size is not worth prosecuting so, instead, the Phamuang used it to exert leverage over the young man. The colonel says that it won't be long before that small-time dealer works his way up the food chain. One day, he might be involved in big shipments, foreign orders, and ice rather than yaba. Until then, his handlers in the Phamuang will keep in touch with him, encouraging him to drip-feed intel. By the time he penetrates deeper into the criminal world, they will already own him.

Is that ethical? It puts the CI in a dangerous situation. How does that make the colonel feel?

'It's a grey area,' he says. 'You have to use your leverage sometimes, but they have to be careful too and they know they can't tell you everything because it will trace back to them. They know enough not to put themselves into a riskier situation.'

I suggest that might not always be true, and I tell him about the dead CI, the one who died working with the

Thai DEA, whose picture I have on my phone. Is that a price worth paying?

'Our CIs don't get killed,' he says. 'The Thai DEA are a little different. From what I see it's usually the smugglers who get killed and not the CIs.'

His reliance on CIs might explain why so few arrests are 'officially' made. Are those apprehended simply enlisted as CIs and sent back? It's certainly plausible. It also strikes me as a situation fraught with risk and danger for other reasons. When there are so many different groups operating as rival mafias who simultaneously share smuggling routes, the potential for all sides to play each other is huge. If I was a smuggler, why wouldn't I manipulate the trigger-happy Thai DEA to do my dirty work for me and take out a rival?

'Yes,' the colonel shrugs, 'sometimes that's a part of it.'

We descend into the colonel's base, settling down around a large hardwood table. The colonel issues an order and immediately four strapping young soldiers come running into the room, each carrying a huge map detailing a section of the border. They are considerably more detailed than any map I've ever seen of the Shan State border areas. They show every hill, every village and every stream for 100 kilometres of river.

The colonel asks me to join him at the first map, which shows clearly the areas bordering Thailand, north of Chiang Mai. There are coloured markers on both sides of the frontier, which he says show the positions of the 509 division of the United Wa State Army (UWSA). The UWSA is the army of the Wa people, an ethnic group who have been at war with the Burmese government for decades. It is widely believed that the Wa are either directly or indirectly involved in the meth trade. It is hard to explain otherwise how so many of the interceptions made by the colonel's force would originate from their territory. I'll speak more about the Wa later but for now it is enough to say that, judging by the colonel's map, the UWSA have a considerable force along this stretch of border, controlling 100 kilometres of territory along the Burmese side of the river. These areas, the colonel says, are the main hotspots for smugglers coming over the Ruak River, and the main sites of gun battles with the Thai DEA.

I wonder how the colonel feels about his men being put in the middle of this murky world, put in the firing line of armed foreign groups, all to clean up a mess that doesn't involve Thailand at all. Drugs produced in Myanmar for consumption in Australia and New Zealand have dragged his men into a war zone.

'The UWSA are only half of the problem,' he says enigmatically. 'Come, I will show you the other.'

It's a thirty-minute drive from the Phamuang base on the Ruak River to Sop Ruak, a small Thai town along the bank of the Mekong River. The river is less than 100 metres across, Laos visible on the other side, scores of small boats crisscrossing in between, heading up and downstream.

At the southern end of town, the SUV pulls up outside a heavily fortified two-storey building. I follow the colonel inside to a room that faces directly across the river. Along a glass wall, I can see across the river to Laos. On the other wall is a bank of CCTV monitors—100 screens showing the river from every single conceivable angle, beaming back the images from hundreds of cameras placed along the Thai side of the river. The colonel shows me how each camera is capable of zooming in to give high-resolution images. With a tweak of a couple of buttons, we can spy on every single person using the river at any time.

The colonel points across the Mekong to a huge building with a golden dome that stands proudly among dozens of half-built multistorey towers on the other side.

'This is Kings Romans,' the colonel says.

The casino? I've heard of Kings Romans. It's a casino in Laos, popular with Chinese tourists.

He nods. 'We know the smugglers use this part of the border to store drugs. Our intel proves that drugs found in Thailand came from here. So now our job is to intercept the drugs before they cross the river.'

I'm as impressed with the sentiment as I am with the technology. The Thai military is demonstrating incredible ambition in its efforts. But looking out across the Mekong now, it strikes me that even with all these cameras, policing a whole river is an impossible task. The Mekong is not the Ruak. It's one of the busiest rivers in the world and any number of these boats could be transporting meth, depositing their cargo anywhere along a 200-kilometre stretch beyond the reach of the cameras.

And yet, the busts keep coming. Thailand seized half a billion yaba pills and 22 tonnes of ice in 2021. Despite all the efforts of the Phamuang and the Thai DEA, with camera surveillance, checkpoints and shootouts, the drugs keep finding a way to Australia.

Along with its neighbour Malaysia, Thailand has become the gateway through which most meth passes on to the rest of the region. Thailand consistently tops the league tables in Asia for quantities of meth seizures, yet production within Thailand is next to nothing. No doubt, Thailand has its own meth problem—yaba pills are so ubiquitous now that the price of a single tablet is less than A$1—but in this regard, Thailand is as much a victim of imported supply as Australia is.

Meanwhile, Thailand is working hard to slow the flow of drugs over its borders, but even with a million cameras, the smugglers would find a way through. The border is too long to be manageable and there's simply too much money to be made to counter industrial levels of corruption.

So why bother? What's the point of this military-grade anti-drug-smuggling operation? The depressing answer seems to be that Thailand needs to be seen to be doing something. Fighting the drug smugglers demonstrates that laws still count for something here. Even if it feels like these efforts are for nothing, just making it a little harder for smugglers, shooting the odd one and occasionally putting a boss in jail stops the flood from becoming a tsunami. It may seem futile but the alternative may be to lose control of everything.

I get the feeling that maybe I'm seeing this situation from the wrong side. The colonel has a great perspective on the trade of ice but, by his own admission, he only sees a fraction of the drugs being transported—the smugglers who stuff up and get caught. To get the full story, I need to cross to the other side of the tracks.

Eventually, I want to see what happens on the other side of the Ruak River, inside Wa territory, for myself. But first, I need to cross the Mekong to investigate what lies beneath that huge golden dome. To understand how meth is smuggled into Thailand I must go to Laos, to Kings Romans, to see for myself who it is that brings the drugs that cross the river into Thailand and where they come from.

4

MY UNCLE IS FUCKED

From the Thai side of the Mekong, Laos is a five-minute boat ride across the slow-flowing, brown waters of South-East Asia's longest river. But before boarding, would-be visitors have to pass through customs and passport control, which operates out of a single-storey, corrugated-iron shack at the edge of the dock. The post is manned by a couple of overweight, sweaty guards in Royal Thai Navy uniforms.

Nearly everyone in the queue is Chinese—male, aged between twenty-five and forty, carrying designer overnight bags, many sporting the latest Premier League football shirts. They remind me of a group of English lads going on a stag do. One tells me that he flew in that morning on a direct flight from China to the local airport in Chiang Rai. Once they get their papers stamped, he says they intend to spend the weekend enjoying all the activities on offer across the river in Kings Romans.

I first heard the name Kings Romans a couple of years ago when a friend told me about a resort that was being built in Laos to cater for Chinese gamblers. Since then, Kings Romans has developed a reputation as a sort of Asian Las Vegas where young men from China can come to let their hair down for a few days.

Kings Romans is one of several new gambling centres established along the Mekong in the last ten years, designed to serve punters from China where gambling is still illegal. According to the UN, these new casinos, unlike the heavily regulated ones in Singapore, offer opportunities not only to weekend gamblers looking for recreation but also to organised criminals seeking to launder profits made from more nefarious activities.

The emergence of casinos in Laos, Cambodia and Vietnam has been mirrored by that of so-called 'junket companies' in Macau. The junkets are rumoured to be run by Chinese triads who spotted a gap in the market. Because the Chinese government, and indeed many inter-national governments, carefully control the flow of money out of their countries by individuals, limits are placed on how much cash you can take abroad with you. The junket companies have been founded to provide a workaround for high rollers making expensive gambling trips overseas.

This is how it works. Say I have US$5 million in my pocket and I decide I want to go and gamble it in a casino in Cambodia or Laos. I can't take $5 million in a suitcase out of the country, nor can I simply wire it to myself because of international money-laundering rules. So instead, I deposit the money with a junket company in Macau for a fee. In exchange, they arrange things so that when I arrive at the casino in Laos, all my accommodation, transport, food, drink and, crucially, gambling credit has been taken care of. That means I have $5 million in credit with the Lao casino to play with, and 100 per cent of any winnings I make on it can be receipted, declared legitimately earned, and then deposited into a nice legit bank account in London or New York. I've taken the dodgy $5 million I earned from drugs or prostitution in Asia and turned it into clean money in the West.

According to the accounts for the NagaWorld casino in Cambodia, which is listed on the Hong Kong stock exchange, the turnover on its high-roller tables in 2019 was more than $45 billion. That's an awful lot of money in a country with a national GDP of only $27 billion.

I don't imagine on this trip that I'll get access to any high rollers or indeed the accounts of the Kings Romans casino, but I want to visit it anyhow—to see the action for myself. I've also heard that this particular town is being used as more than just a dirty-money laundry. It's also an important stop on the Meth Road.

With my passport stamped, I file onto a longtail taxi-boat to make the crossing. The skyline is filled with cranes and construction sites. I count more than forty towers at various stages of completion. At the centre of it all is the glistening golden dome, which reminds me of the temple of Jerusalem. The taxi-boat operator informs me that it belongs to the main hall of the Kings Romans casino. Adjacent to it is a vast monolith, which he says is the new hotel. Standing more than forty storeys high, it has in excess of 1000 bedrooms. Someone is planning for an invasion of people and has already begun working out where to put them all.

Although technically still within the sovereign state of the Lao People's Democratic Republic, Kings Romans is an autonomous economic zone with its own border controls. After paying an entrance fee and receiving another new passport stamp, I jump into a cab for the short drive into town, noting the shops, the street names, the billboards advertising phone networks—everything is written in Chinese. There's not a word of the Lao language to be seen.

Kings Romans is the brainchild of Chinese billionaire Zhao Wei, currently sanctioned by the US Treasury for his alleged involvement in an international drug-trafficking ring. Originally from northern China, Zhao Wei made his money in timber before he moved into casinos, first in Macau, China, and then later in Mong La, a nearby district of eastern Myanmar.

Ten years ago, with a billion dollars in the bank, Zhao decided that operating casinos in other people's territories and having to play by their rules was an inconvenience he could do without. He contacted the Lao government and proposed that in return for an undisclosed envelope of cash, he would take 3000 hectares of land in the north of the country on a ninety-nine-year lease. The Laos agreed and Zhao began building Kings Romans.

After checking into the hotel, I walk down to the casino to take a look around. I'm starting to feel more like I'm in a Chinese resort than a Lao city. Everyone here is Chinese—the punters, the waiters, the croupiers. They speak to each other in Mandarin as they place their bets on baccarat tables, a typical Chinese gambling game. They smoke Chinese cigarettes and order Chinese snacks. The only sign of anything foreign is the Johnnie Walker being served at the bar.

The area in which Kings Romans is located is called the Golden Triangle Special Economic Zone. It was once agricultural land. The inhabitants of Ban Kwan, the village that stood in the middle of the economic zone, were 'relocated' to make way for the development. Their appeals fell on deaf ears as they were unceremoniously packed up and shipped off elsewhere by their government.

Anyone who did remain in the economic zone after the mass evictions now lives under Zhao Wei's rules. There is no Lao authority here at all. The Special Economic Zone is entirely self-policing; its smartly uniformed police officers can be seen patrolling the streets, and it has its own private fleet of ambulances and fire trucks. Although you don't have to spend much time here to realise that the enforcement of the law is rather looser than it is in most other places.

When I finally get out of the casino, I take a walk up the street, past a group of local guys playing a jumpers-for-goalposts game of football in a small park. I spot what looks like a row of cages protruding from behind some bushes on the far side of the pitch and discover, to my surprise, that the cages contain around twenty fully grown tigers. With nobody else around, I can walk right up to them, unencumbered, close enough that I could, if I felt inclined, reach right through the bars to touch them. They eyeball me with suspicion from the other side of the bars. Piles of decaying chicken carcasses are scattered across the stone floor, providing evidence that at least someone is feeding them. Who that might be is not clear.

I've heard rumours that there are places in this zone where you can dine on tiger meat, or drink tiger bone wine distilled from the skeletons of the animals, which is 'guaranteed' to increase your libido. Very little has ever been proven and one report published by the Environmental Investigation Agency, which claimed that tiger meat and tiger bone wine were widely available in Kings Romans' restaurants, has been denied vehemently by the authorities. But seeing twenty tigers caged in the park opposite the casino does make me wonder if I have inadvertently stumbled across a farm.

When I enquire at the local Chinese restaurant that evening if tiger meat might be on the menu, the waiter shakes his head.

'There are no tigers in Kings Romans,' he says.

'But I saw some today,' I say. 'In the park.'

'No, that is not possible,' he replies before he asks me to leave.

Strolling back through town, the place has come alive for the night. Here are crowds of Chinese men like the ones I saw at the border. Puddles on the street glow pink, reflecting neon signs advertising girly bars and brothels on both sides of the street. Prostitutes are openly available. I grab a taxi and the driver asks if she can take me somewhere 'special', which makes my ears prick up. *Why not?* Kings Romans has spiked my interest. I tell her that I've had a lucky day in the casino, so she should feel free to take me somewhere I can celebrate.

She drops me outside of a large building with huge wooden doors at least 6 metres high. I pass into a dark foyer and head up a double staircase that leads up to a corridor high above. I can hear the sound of dance music and, as my eyes adjust to the darkness, I notice a young Chinese man with a girl sitting on his knee. He does a double-take as I walk past, along the corridor towards the music, until it opens out into a bar area.

More Chinese guys are chatting with young girls inside. Everyone looks a bit stunned to see a white guy, and I spot one of the girls scurrying off into a back room with an urgency that suggests my arrival may have triggered some kind of alarm. It's pretty dark inside, so working out the precise age of the girls is hard, but I'd say fifteen or sixteen would be a reasonable guess. They're all of a type: painfully thin and very well groomed, not like the street girls in the brothels and girly bars outside.

Next to the bar is another door, which I push open. Inside, there are two Chinese guys and ten very young girls. One of the guys has his shirt off and is ballroom dancing with a girl I guess is no more than thirteen years old. She's tiny and thin, her pale skin almost shining under the dim pink light above. The other guy is reclining in a chaise longue while two similarly petite girls stroke his chest and kiss him on the nipples.

At once, everyone freezes. All eyes on me. A second later the door bursts open again, and this time a crowd of angry-looking Chinese men pile inside.

'What is wrong with you?' a particularly angry-looking guy screams.

'I was looking for somewhere to get a drink,' I say innocently. 'Do you have any tiger bone wine?'

'No. You must leave now,' he orders.

'How old are these girls?' I ask.

'Get out, now!' he growls. 'Or there will be big trouble.'

I walk back to my hotel, where there are now several more prostitutes sitting around in the foyer—waiting to be called by men staying in the rooms upstairs, perhaps. It all feels pretty sordid and incredibly brazen. There's no attempt to conceal what is happening in this city of vice. Animal meat, gambling and underage sex are all available for a price as long as you meet one condition—you have to be Chinese. Maybe it's a suspicion of Westerners that makes me persona non grata around here, but it's obvious all this 'entertainment' isn't meant for me.

The next day, I call Alessandro Rippa, an academic and China specialist who I know spent some time in Kings Romans researching his PhD. Places like Kings Romans are cropping up all across South-East Asia, in what Alessandro believes is the modern-day equivalent of what the historian Willem van Schendel called 'Zomia'—a place that exists outside of state-run institutions, where quasi-societies of multi-ethnic, non-hierarchical populations can come together to escape the power of the state.

'I think it's possible today to live outside of national laws if you have enough money,' Alessandro says, 'but you can't do it here without the support of China.'

In 2018, Zhao's criminal organisation in Kings Romans was exposed in the *South China Morning Post*. Kings Romans is Zhao Wei's private patch of Zomia—an independent state created by a special 'elite' individual who has decided that he no longer wants to live by anyone else's laws. But Alessandro argues that Zhao still needs to keep the powers that be on the Chinese side of the border happy. As long as he can do that, then he's left alone to run his private tiger-eating, child-abusing, online-gambling, drug-smuggling empire exactly the way he sees fit, generating licit profit through illicit means.

What I've seen in Kings Romans myself supports the idea that there is little regard for international law in this place. Kings Romans seems to be designed and ruled over by a powerful Chinese billionaire who can afford to create his own kingdom. Alessandro calls this 'Zomia 2.0'. The rules are set by Zhao and enforced by his private police force with a light touch. Activities such as eating endangered animals and engaging in child prostitution are condemned in the rest of the world but openly tolerated here. It's not a stretch to imagine how that wilful blind eye could be turned away from the drug trade too.

The problem for the rest of the world is that, if what the UN is saying about this place is true, then what happens in Kings Romans has a global impact. This is not a victimless crime. If the trade in amphetamines does pass directly through here then its impact is being felt on the streets of Manila, Seoul and Sydney. What I need to prove to myself now is whether that is the case.

The concerning fact is that Kings Romans is not unique. Alessandro has identified other parts of Zomia in Myanmar—one in Mong La and another in Pangkham. I too had previously seen something similar several years before in the casino town of Boten, 300 kilometres from here. It was while I was researching my book *Unfair Trade* that I first realised that self-administering casino towns existed at all. There, I wrote of the systematic deforestation of northern Laos by unscrupulous Chinese timber merchants and some associated rubber companies. My research uncovered that Lao's political leaders were secretly taking backhanders in return for turning a blind eye to the rape of the country's resources by their unscrupulous neighbours.

While researching that book, I enlisted the help of a young activist called Bounsing, who helped me to access areas of the rainforest where those private Chinese enterprises were quietly deforesting valuable hardwoods away from the prying eyes of regulators. As I was back in the area, I decided to drop him a line and see what he was up to.

———

Bounsing looks well when he collects me from a river port, 80 or so kilometres further along the Mekong from Kings Romans, in a brand-new Chinese four-wheel drive. It's nearly ten years since we first met but he still looks the same—slender and handsome, a bluff of wiry black hair spouting from his chin. As we take the road north towards Luang Namtha and the northern Lao border, he fills me in on how his life has changed. He's now married with a baby on the way and a steady job.

'I work for a Chinese company now,' he says.

'*What?*' I can't believe it. This was a guy who ten years ago would rather have died in a ditch than work for the enemy.

'Yeah, I know,' he chuckles, 'but the Chinese are the only ones with jobs for Lao people. No Lao company will employ me.'

Bounsing's vehicle makes good time on the newly tracked Chinese-built road through the hills that rise on either side of us as we pass into the national park. A sign to our left reads 'Nam Ha National Protected Area', but evidence of the lack of protection is everywhere to see. The indigenous forest has been systematically cleared away to make space for rubber trees. The effect on the hillside is clear and stark; hundreds and hundreds of rows of bare trunks climb up and over the hills into the distance like the skeletal remains of a decaying carcass.

'When you were here last, the price of rubber was five dollars per kilo,' Bounsing says, 'so many people cut down their trees and planted rubber to get rich.'

Now the price of Lao rubber is nearer to 50 cents a kilo. 'You need thirty trees to make one kilo but even a good worker can only cover three or four hundred trees in one night,' says Bounsing. 'The workers only get forty per cent of that price.'

What he's saying means that an eight-hour shift in the Lao rubber plantations will earn a manual worker two or three US dollars. The price of rubber on the other side of the border in Myanmar, he says, is even less. 'The Hmong people, who live up in the forests around here,' says Bounsing, scanning the hillside, 'they cannot make a living from this kind of work anymore.'

During the Vietnam War, the CIA enlisted the Hmong people to fight on their side against the North Vietnamese communists. As an ancient hill people, the

Hmong knew the forests of Laos and Vietnam better than anyone—they could find routes through the jungle nobody else knew, which made them great trackers and spies. For the duration of the war, thousands of young Hmong men signed up to fight against the North Vietnamese; later, their leader Vang Pao doubled down against communism and led the Hmong people in the fight against the Lao communist government. Problem is that both times, the Hmong backed the wrong side and so, once Lao established a communist government in Vientiane, many Hmong had to flee—abroad for the lucky ones who could get asylum, back to the forest for those who couldn't.

Bounsing isn't Hmong, he's Tai Lue, one of a lowland tribe whose lands border Hmong territory. Bounsing explains that while Tai Lue and Hmong have no historical beef with each other, until very recently the Hmong and Lao people remained sworn enemies. However, things are changing as recently the Lao government has started working hard to welcome the Hmong back into the Lao fold and extend rights equal to Lao people in their society.

As we emerge out of the national park, the road flattens out and we soon arrive in the town where Bounsing grew up—Muang Sing.

'Welcome to smuggler-town,' he laughs.

Before I can ask him what he means, we pass a huge house. Like, palatial huge. It's three storeys high, 100 metres from end to end, and covered in spectacular bright-green tiles, as is the fashion in this part of the world. The whole property is surrounded by a 6-metre-high chrome fence, lined in razor wire.

'You should see his house in Vientiane,' says Bounsing. 'It's twice that size.'

'It belongs to a smuggler?' I ask.

'One of the biggest,' he nods.

Historically, the town of Muang Sing was a major link in the trade of opium through the northern Lao region. Bounsing says that it's maintained its position as a 'smuggler-town' as the drug trade has evolved. He says that the town's geographical proximity to both China and Myanmar still makes it the perfect place from which to run an international drug-running operation. He's bringing me here to meet with his father, Po, because last year Po's brother—Bounsing's uncle—was caught and arrested for smuggling over 100 kilograms of crystal methamphetamine into the Lao capital Vientiane. He's been in prison awaiting his sentence ever since.

'He will get the death penalty,' says Bounsing. 'My uncle is . . .' he pauses, looking for the right English word.

'Fucked?' I offer.

'Yes,' he says, with a smile of sad resignation on his face. 'My uncle is fucked.'

We pull up outside a more modest detached modern house; this is the house where Bounsing explains he grew up. I'm impressed. It's not nearly as large as the palace we just passed but by no means a modest dwelling either.

'What did you say your dad did for a living?' I ask.

'He was a trader,' says Bounsing. 'Buffalos and rice.'

Bounsing gets out of the car to greet his father while I wonder how many buffalos you'd have to sell to buy a place this size. The two men embrace. They haven't seen each other in over a year, not since Bounsing took his job at the Chinese company.

Po is a slightly built man in his sixties with kind brown eyes and thinning black hair. He invites us to sit and we make small talk while Bounsing's mother busies herself on the other side of the yard boiling a pot of buffalo skin. She looks up for just a moment to acknowledge me with a nod and a broad, jolly smile while Bounsing and his father talk animatedly in their dialect. Po keeps pointing to another big house across the street.

'That's where my best friend lived,' Bounsing says with a sad shake of his head. 'He's in jail now too, waiting on the death penalty. The family need six hundred million kip to get him out but they won't pay.' Six hundred million Lao kip at the time was worth about US$67,000.

'A bribe?' I ask.

'Yes.'

For those who can afford it, the corruption machine extends to death row in Laos.

Over a cup of green tea, Bounsing explains to Po the purpose of my visit. The old man considers what his son is saying carefully before he suggests we take a drive down to the river at Xieng Kok, a nearby port where traders like Po have long exploited its proximity to China to move goods back and forth along the river. For years Lao traders have been taking advantage of the higher prices paid in the Chinese markets of Yunnan province. Back when Po was still working, buffalo and rice were the growth markets but now he says it's chicken innards and energy drinks that are making the 'big bucks'. I nod but

I feel like we both know where the really big bucks are being made—and it isn't Red Bull and giblets.

Bounsing says that his father has a friend in Xieng Kok who might be interesting for me to meet, but when he translates this idea for his father, the two men begin to talk animatedly again in their own tongue. Finally, Bounsing explains to me that his father says it would be better if we pretend that I am a drug dealer from Australia. He says his friend will be more interested to talk if he thinks that I am here on business—maybe looking to cut out the middleman from my supply chain. Ironically, if my reason for being in 'smuggler-town' is to source drugs, then I will be regarded with less suspicion.

'It's better this way,' Bounsing says.

We get back in the car and, cast in my new role as an Aussie meth dealer, we head off to a meeting along the banks of the Mekong river with Po's contact.

The road to Xieng Kok is dusty and unsealed, riddled with bumps and potholes. We pass heavily loaded Chinese lorries along the way. I can't help but wonder if any might be loaded up with drugs bound for international markets. It seems Po might be sharing the same thoughts because he turns and starts to talk to me.

'When I was a boy, there was no amphetamine here,' he says. 'Only poppy. The mountain people would smoke it. But then they began to bring yaba here and everything changed.'

The arrival of drugs in the town brought in new money and a new spate of social problems too. Crime in Muang Sing used to be unheard of but now he says petty thievery is common.

'Some people invested, bought boats, got involved in the drug business and got rich,' Po says. 'When someone builds a big house here, we can suspect where the money comes from.'

I wonder if he suspects that any of that new money is coming from the production of amphetamines.

'No,' he shakes his head. 'We don't produce here. Only smuggle. The smugglers here have networks in Myanmar with the big bosses. They even come here sometimes.'

'The producers come to Muang Sing?'

'Before my brother was arrested, he met with his big boss at my house. They shared out their money there.'

I'm amazed that Po has come face to face with the producers themselves. From what Bounsing has told me, Po's brother was no small fish. He was caught with over 100 kilograms of ice.

'The guys who came to your house—who were they?' I ask.

'Wa,' he says. 'They were Wa.'

We don't stop in Xieng Kok but instead continue along the Mekong until Po directs Bounsing to pull onto a long dusty track. Goats and chickens scurry across the road and dirty children peer into the vehicle. I get the impression that few vehicles pass through here, especially ones containing white people. At the end of the track is a small restaurant that sits on the hill overlooking Xieng Kok's number one landmark—the Myanmar–Lao Friendship Bridge, completed in May 2015.

Officially, the bridge is still closed to crossings, but despite that fact, I can see a motorcycle setting off from the Myanmar side, slowly making its way across the river. It's a curious sight to see one solitary vehicle on a four-lane bridge. When it reaches the Lao side, it pulls up alongside a fence that separates us from the bridge and then, with no regard for the soldiers manning the Lao checkpoint right in front of us, two figures climb off and hop over the fence.

We sit down to talk in the empty restaurant. Bounsing translates for me, explaining that the pair are a husband-and-wife smuggling team, operating from Kenglat in Myanmar. As they are ethnically Tai Lue and loosely related to Bounsing and his father, we can talk freely. Po, in turn, vouches for me, while Bounsing bigs me up as an important man in the Australian drug world. He explains that I have come from Australia to discuss a potential deal.

It's hard to tell what level of danger I'm facing. Are these people armed? What would be the consequences if they suspected I was lying? I have no idea but, all things considered, I figure it's better not to find out. So, I stick to my cover story and tell them that over the last couple of months, I've been developing contacts in the region. I say that I have found a source of high-quality product but my challenge now is how to move that product to Australia. They listen quietly, nodding as though this is a common problem. Finally, the man begins to speak.

'We have no experience to move product to Australia,' he says, 'but we can move to the Thai border . . . at Kings Romans.'

I suggest that 100 kilograms of ice would be a good start. A test that we can work together. The man shrugs as though this is nothing and reassures me that he can deliver that quantity of ice to me at Kings Romans casino, no problem. I tell him I'm still worried about the logistics of delivery.

'The drugs go by boat,' he says. Then, after a short discussion with his wife, he explains: 'The boat owner charges us for the transfer fee and we have to pay off the officials and the border checks. We have to pay many bribes.' The total fee, he says, is 100,000 Thai baht, or A$4000, per kilo.

Wow. My first thought is that it's cheap. At that price, surely it wouldn't be long before the price of a gram began to drop on the streets of Sydney too. It seems less about the power of authorities to stop the trade and more about the simple economic reality of oversupply. Look at the rubber. It's the same. When supply outstrips demand, prices fall into the dirt.

The smuggler says the other advantage of delivering the drugs to Kings Romans is that we avoid the Lao authorities.

'That zone is easy for us,' he says. 'We have a good network there and we trust them. The casino people are not directly involved, they take the bribe and don't ask for anything. We don't need to consider about the security. There is no army, no police.'

I wonder if he can introduce me to anyone who could help me move the drugs on from there, reminding him that my final destination is Australia and not a casino town in Laos. The question prompts an animated discussion between them.

'I recommend you go to meet with a guy in the village near to Kings Romans. The guy there is super rich and he has a big house and another big house in the capital.'

I ask Bounsing if he knows the place the man is talking about.

'Tonpheung,' he replies.

'Yes. That is the same village,' the man confirms. 'The guy there can help you to move the product to the place where you want.'

'Can you introduce us?'

I hear him floating the idea to his wife: 'Let's introduce them, and if the business is a success then we'll get our commission.'

But she has other ideas. She explains that in the past they have overlapped with the Hmong boss, whose network runs their drugs from Kings Romans into Thailand, but as far as making that connection goes, she wants to see how we proceed together first.

'So how can we proceed?' I ask.

'That's up to you,' she replies. 'Take your time, no problem. Let us know when you are ready.'

They leave the way they came, over the fence and along the deserted bridge on their motorbike. We get back in the four-wheel drive and head back to the port in Xieng Kok, where I find a boat to take me back along the Mekong River to Kings Romans. Today I have made an important link along the Meth Road. If I did have a quantity of methamphetamine in Myanmar, and I needed to move it, then I now know how to move it as far as the lawless Kings Romans and, from there, potentially to a port in Thailand.

I thank my old friend and his father again for all their help, waving them goodbye as our little riverboat drifts away from the bank a little after 3 p.m. We follow the slow current along the mighty Mekong with Laos to our left,

Myanmar to our right. There are points at which the river is so narrow that you could throw a stone across from one country to the other. We pass boats travelling in both directions, running cargo between China and the surrounding areas. Many are large enough to carry several containers, any one of which could easily be concealing a tonne of ice.

The sun falls fast out of the sky, casting the river into darkness and my boat's captain pulls into a sandy beach on the Laos side of the river. We're still a couple of hours from Kings Romans so we have to make camp here until the sun returns—the river is not navigable in the dark. I make a campfire from driftwood I find on the beach, and the captain offers me a thin blanket and a packet of dried noodles. It's basic but it feels exciting to be camping wild, free, along what is certainly part of the Meth Road. Out here there are no authorities, no Phamuang, no DEA. It's no wonder that the river is the smugglers' preferred route.

The next morning, the captain gets the boat back on the river and delivers me to Kings Romans. I take a taxi to the border crossing, past the golden dome of the casino and the park across the street, noting that the tiger cages have gone, cleared away, the evidence destroyed and the tigers moved to a more discreet location.

I feel as though I've taken an important step back along the Meth Road, a step closer to linking the markets of Australia to the supply in Asia. Kings Romans is a vital step along that path, providing not only laundered cash flow for the trade in amphetamines but a safe harbour for the drugs themselves. Somewhere there is a bonded warehouse, safe from international law, where meth can be imported from Myanmar and stored until it is ready to be transported across Thailand, then to the seaports and onto the ships that will carry it south to Australia.

It also makes it very clear to me where I am heading next. According to the smugglers, all the meth that is passing through Kings Romans into Thailand is coming from one place and one place only—Myanmar. It is time that I went there for myself and found out who is supplying the smugglers. I would have loved to have accompanied the husband-and-wife team I met in Xieng Kok across the Friendship Bridge but that route is closed to foreigners. Instead, I must cross the river back into Thailand, retrace my steps to Chiang Rai and take the road that heads north to Myanmar and the border crossing at a town called Tachileik.

5

DO NOT TRUST YOUR KNEE

The bus from Chiang Rai to the Myanmar border takes about an hour and passes through lush, thick rainforest. In the Thai town of Mae Sai, the road disappears through a series of barriers into a no-man's-land of customs and passport controls. Tourists line up along the pavement to make the short walk over the bridge into what is still one of the world's least visited places. Most have no intention of going very far once they reach the other side. They're passport-stamp collectors, dipping their cautious toes into Myanmar for an hour or two, a little adventure on an otherwise cosy vacation—pop over, pick up a souvenir and go home, saying 'Been to Myanmar, bought the t-shirt.'

No doubt, Myanmar's notoriety has been created by the country's chequered past. For the last sixty years, its people have been mired in various iterations of civil war, all the while ruled over by a cruel military junta, while the sole spokesperson for democracy and change, Aung San Suu Kyi, has been sidelined in a cell or under house arrest. It's easy to understand why a tourist from Arkansas might consider a trip over the border, however fleeting, to be an act of wanton courageousness.

For my part, I've been dying to get into Myanmar since I met the smugglers on the other side of the Friendship Bridge. I have a good understanding now of the route that Australia's meth takes from Asia. The sea routes from big international ports in Thailand and Malaysia are the primary arteries down which drugs are being pumped into Sydney's and Melbourne's suburbs. The drugs arrive there by way of a network of Asian smuggling gangs who transport them through their areas of control, using lawless fiefdoms such as Kings Romans as important staging posts along the way. But before that, before the ice ever hits the Meth Road, it's produced somewhere by people who have the necessary means and expertise.

I follow the tourists over the bridge into Shan State and lay my bag down on the dusty road to get a measure of where I am. Tachileik is the name of the border town on this side of the Ruak River, sitting opposite its twin, Mae Sai on the Thai side. The river here is shallow and narrow, perfect for smugglers to easily pass across to the other side at any number of points. In front of me, sitting in the middle of the traffic island is a statue proclaiming that Tachileik is the 'City of the Golden Triangle'.

The Golden Triangle area is legendary in the world of drugs. The term was first coined by the CIA in the 1950s and while technically it's the name given to the point where the nations of Myanmar, Thailand and Laos meet at the confluence of the Mekong and Ruak rivers, it's more widely used to describe the hundreds of thousands of square kilometres of surrounding jungle that have produced much of the world's opium for the last couple of hundred years.

The opium poppy was introduced to the region by Chinese traders in the mid-eighteenth century. Gradually it was adopted by ethnic groups for medicinal and recreational uses and it grew well in the fertile lands surrounding the Mekong. As the demand for heroin exploded internationally, opium cultivation in Myanmar and its neighbouring countries, Thailand and Laos, expanded in step until the region became the number one producer of opium poppy in the world.

Today, opium is still grown widely in Shan State. During times of conflict, it can be hard for farmers to access traditional markets for agricultural product but the criminal groups come and buy opium from the farm gate. Since the coup in 2020, movement has become even more restricted and so it's no surprise that opium production has started to rise again. Despite this, Myanmar's opium production is still dwarfed by Afghanistan which, according to the UNODC, supplies over 90 per cent of the global heroin market.

Motorbikes whizz around me and street vendors tug at my shoulder, hawking knock-off Rolexes, encouraging me to follow them into the labyrinthine street market that has been laid on for the daytrippers. The sound is intense as a steady stream of traffic passes by, horns beeping, people yelling, and the general early evening chaos that takes place in most Asian cities. A young woman whizzes past me on her bike, carrying an umbrella, which, as it is nearly 6 p.m. and not raining, leaves me scratching my head.

The only taxis in evidence here are motorcycle taxis. Twenty or so men in high-vis yellow bibs line up next to the roundabout, watching the passers-by intently, ready to jump on the chance of a fare. One driver pushes his motorcycle in my direction. He is skinny and balding, and stands at about 5 foot 2. His face is dark, his eyes bright and before he speaks, he spits a huge dollop of red betel nut onto the street between us. 'Hello,' he says, 'My name is Michael. Where are you going?'

I perch on the back of Michael's bike, and we weave through the Tachileik traffic towards my hotel. He turns his head around intermittently to talk to me over his shoulder. I wish he wouldn't. Every time his eyes dart back in my direction, I brace myself for impact. He seems happy to risk our lives while he tells me all the things I can find in Tachileik.

First, Michael offers to procure me a prostitute, which I politely decline. He then offers to take me to the casino, as though he's running through a list of vices looking for the right one. I decide to see if his list extends as far as drugs.

'Ice?' I ask.

'Ice?' he checks. 'Yes. Yaba, ice, opium, heroin. Everything. But not cocaine. Cocaine I cannot get.'

He delivers me safely to my hotel and promises to call me that evening. I'm evasive when he asks me what I'm in town for. A Western face sticks out like a sore thumb in a town like Tachileik and I'm not sure I can trust him yet. After he leaves, I take a walk back along the street to the market, a collection of stalls covered in cloth awnings, selling more fake watches, tourist t-shirts and street food. Around me, a smattering of tourists browses the items for sale.

At the end of a quiet street, I see a sign for the Allure Resort, a huge white-and-gold hotel adorned with Roman pillars. There's a fountain out front flanked by two grand dragon statues. A man approaches me, carrying a basket of cigarette packets and blue pills. 'Viagra? Cialis?' he whispers under his breath, the first visible sign that Tachileik has more to offer visitors than fake Rolexes and bad food. In May 2019, 188 Chinese nationals were arrested at two separate hotels in town. The police seized guns and ammo, drugs, walkie-talkies and hundreds of mobile phones. The charge made against the individuals was that they were responsible for a huge drug-trafficking operation, running meth into Thailand.

Inside the hotel, the mood feels quiet and sombre. Nobody at the reception desk even acknowledges me as I take the stairs to the first floor, where I get the faint whiff of bitter cigarette smoke dampened slightly by the air conditioning. Behind a large gold door at the end of the corridor is a casino hall. This is not Las Vegas. There are no pontoon tables, no craps and no high rollers sipping on free cocktails. Instead, there is an assortment of poker machines pushed up against a wall, and a couple of empty baccarat tables in the middle of the room. The clientele is entirely Thai, lower-working-class men and women, betting peanuts and smoking cigarettes while they plough small-denomination chips into the pokies. Nobody here seems likely to be connected to the meth business.

Later that evening, Michael calls by and says that tomorrow he will take me to meet a dealer he knows who sells large quantities of ice and has connections to providers within Myanmar. I've been in Tachileik for less than a day and already it seems I've made inroads into tracking down contacts in the industry.

———

The following morning, the sun feels hot before the clock has struck eight. Michael pulls up outside the café where we've agreed to meet. He seems in a funny mood today, a little distracted and irritable, and there seems to be something different about his motorcycle. I'm not really into motorcycles, so at first I wonder if he's just replaced his old seat cover. Then I realise he's driving a completely different motorcycle.

Did he get a new bike?

'It is my wife's,' he says.

Where was his motorcycle?

'It is in the repair. Two thousand baht to fix it.' He looks pissed off.

Did he have a crash?

'Yes. Last night. I crashed into the fence.'

Was he drunk?

'Yes.'

He giggles a little as he takes a seat and orders himself a beer. It's quiet in the café; only a few of the tables are occupied but still Michael scans each patron carefully, assessing every one of them until he is happy that nobody is listening to our conversation.

I'm interested in how he ended up in Tachileik. He's one of the very few people I've met here who speaks English fluently. Michael explains that he was the seventh child of nine, born in a village in Kayah State, the state to the south-west of Shan, where the people are mostly indigenous Karenni. His father was the headman of the village.

'There is a proverb in Myanmar,' Michael says. 'If you chop down the wrong tree in the forest, you have bad luck for one year, but if you marry the wrong woman, you have bad luck for the rest of your life.'

Facing the very real prospect of economic hardship for his people, Michael's dad reluctantly made the decision that their village could no longer afford not to grow opium. The conflict with the Myanmar Army had flared up again in Kayah State and crop prices fell sharply. Villages, desperate for money, began to cash in on the growing international demand for heroin by converting their wheat fields to opium poppy. One morning, when Michael was seven years old, his father went into the forest with an axe and ceremoniously chopped down the largest tree he could find to signify that, from then on, their village was in the opium business.

'That year,' Michael says before taking another swig of beer, 'four of my siblings died.'

While I try to process that information, Michael continues with his story, explaining how, within weeks of the tree falling in the forest, he lost his eldest sister in childbirth and another sister to a fatal snake bite; then a brother died fighting the war and, finally, his eldest brother perished when (ironically) another tree fell in the forest and crushed him to death.

But before the year was out, more tragedy struck Michael's family. Later that year, he says a group of Karenni rebel militia came to his village and asked his father to hide them. They'd suffered heavy casualties in a fight with the Myanmar Army and needed time to regroup before they retreated to join the rest of their forces. The army, hot on their trail, turned up in the village the following day, took Michael's father away and tortured him until he agreed to show them where the rebels were hiding.

Michael's father had no choice but to lead the army to the rebels' hiding place. In the skirmish that followed, most of the rebels were killed. Only a few managed to escape.

Weeks later, the rebels returned with reinforcements to find the village headman who had given up their position.

'They took my father into the forest,' Michael says. 'They tied him to a tree and then they eat him.'

I'm sure I've misheard. 'You mean they killed him?'

Michael shakes his head and repeats what he just said. There's no mistaking it this time. He mimes putting food in his mouth. He says the rebels tore his father's flesh from his bones, and then, in front of his father's eyes, took turns to eat it. Finally, they left him to bleed to death.

'They did it to put fear in the people's hearts,' says Michael. 'When we find my father's body in the jungle, we know why they have done this thing.'

There have been many unconfirmed allegations of atrocities committed by soldiers in Myanmar, and suggestions that both sides of the conflict have committed cannibalism by eating the hearts and livers of their enemies in Shan and Kayah. The Wa, too, who live not far from Michael's village, were for a long time renowned as the Wild Wa for their human-flesh-eating practices.

I've always taken these stories with a pinch of salt. I've seen atrocities committed in some terrible places in my career, not least in the Democratic Republic of the Congo, where rape and murder of civilians are common occurrences at the hands of intoxicated rebel soldiers in the deep jungles. But consuming human flesh seems too horrific for my brain to reconcile.

Whatever the truth of it, the result was that after his family's year of tragedy, his mother could no longer support the family and so seven-year-old Michael and his remaining two brothers were sent away. It was decided that Michael would go to a Christian missionary school run by the Jesuits, where he was taught English, Latin and Mathematics.

Against the odds, young Michael thrived and, when he was seventeen, he came sixth out of the 22,000 students who sat national exams. He qualified for a scholarship at the Jesuit seminary and was sent to Perth, Australia, to study for the priesthood.

Now, Michael is clearly not a priest, so something went wrong with that plan. He giggles again as he tells me how, within six months of landing in Australia, he was caught 'socialising' with local women on more than one occasion. The Jesuits expelled him from the priesthood and sent him back to Myanmar in disgrace. Skint, and with no life to return to, Michael decided that the border town of Tachileik was where his talents could be best put to use.

Although nominally a motorcycle taxi driver, he says that he now moonlights as a 'fixer' for tourists looking to partake in the seedier activities available in town. His shopping list of Tachileik's recreational activities includes all the drugs and also a smorgasbord of sexual options, which includes girls as young as fourteen, the legal age of consent in Myanmar.

'But even a virgin I can find,' he boasts. 'For the right price, anything is possible here.'

I'm horrified at the suggestion.

'Two thousand US dollars,' he says, before I ask.

He answers his ringing phone and grunts into it a few times before hanging up. He downs his beer and bounces out of his seat. Moments later, I'm back on his motorcycle, weaving in and out of the Tachileik traffic again.

———

The town is arranged along one main street, 5 or 6 kilometres long, like an artery conveying all the life and oxygen on which the town thrives. Cafés sit next to pharmacies and grocery stores in between the noodle stalls and beer stations. Everywhere, I can see the green-and-red logo of the nation's beer, imaginatively called 'Myanmar', along with the phone carriers Ooredoo and Mytel.

Michael stops at a corner stall to buy some fresh betel nut, which he tucks into his cheek. His teeth are already covered in red stains, as if he is a freshly fed vampire. My dental hygienist would have a coronary if she saw the state of them. Back on the bike, I feel the moment when the stimulant kicks in because he suddenly drives a lot faster.

We turn off the main road, up a hill, past a group of addicts sitting by the side of the road, openly injecting drugs into their arms. The houses up here are bigger— two-storey, gated, surrounded by high walls.

Tachileik is a constant surprise to me. Every time I think I have the measure of it, there's another area that I hadn't realised was there. It's a city of 55,000 souls but because all the commerce is located down a single street, some of its outskirts go on for miles.

We reach a row of two-storey concrete buildings where the ground floor is made up of shops—a beauty salon, a noodle shop and another brightly lit storefront. Michael hops off the bike and tells me to follow him inside.

In the middle of the room is a machine, and I've never seen anything like it before: about three by two metres, the height of a snooker table, topped with a large, flat LCD screen. The screen is lit up with images of aquatic animals swimming back and forth, like looking down into a digital aquarium. Standing around the edge of the 'pool' are three young men who are rapidly pushing buttons that seem to fire rockets at the passing fish. Every time a carp or an octopus explodes, they gather points.

A short, ethnically Chinese guy appears and introduces himself to me as Luke. Luke is early-middle-aged, thick-set, with short black hair and a lazy gait. He wears a Manchester United football shirt, stonewashed jeans and a pair of thongs, and I'm sure that I can pick up a distinctly American twang in his accent. He lights a cigarette and watches me with interest as I try to make sense of the game.

'You never see this game before?' he asks. 'Yeah, it's a lot of fun, man. You can play . . .'

'Maybe after we talk,' I say.

'Okay, yeah cool,' he says. 'Let's go upstairs.'

———

It's impossible to understand why South-East Asia is the epicentre of the Australian meth epidemic today without first understanding the deep-rooted historical forces that forged its current situation. To best illustrate that for you, I'd like to take you back fifty years to an incident, a battle of sorts that was waged in a quiet clearing in the Lao jungle between competing forces intent on seizing control of the global heroin trade. This may seem anachronistic to our journey along the Meth Road but bear with me: one could not exist without the other.

That journey began in June 1967 when 200 heavily loaded mules plodded south through the monsoon downpours towards Ban Houei Sai, a Lao town along the Mekong river, 40 kilometres as the crow files from where Kings Romans now stands. The convoy was ferrying 16 tonnes of opium but as it rolled onwards, it was joined by smaller caravans appearing out of the jungle, also carrying consignments of the drug from surrounding market towns until, by the time it reached the Thai–Lao border, its single-file column of 500 men and 300 mules stretched beyond the ridge line for several kilometres, intent on delivering nearly 20 tonnes of raw opium to a heroin factory across the border.

The man in charge of the operation was a half-Chinese, half-Shan rebel who went by the name Chang Chi-fu. One day he would be better known as the notorious drug lord

Khun Sa. Khun Sa was born on 17 February 1934 to a Chinese father and a Shan mother. When he was three, his father died and his mother abandoned him to marry a local tax collector, leaving the young boy to be raised by his Shan grandfather in a jungle village called Loi Maw, deep in the Shan Hills.

By the time he turned fourteen, Khun Sa had given up on school and joined a military training camp run by the Kuomintang, a group of Chinese rebels who had ruled China until they were beaten in a bloody civil war by Mao's Communist Party in 1949. As the Kuomintang retreated, they disbanded into two groups, one fleeing over the sea to Taiwan in the east, the other over the jungle border to Shan State, Burma. In Taiwan, they brutally took over the island, suppressing local resistance, establishing themselves as the new political order in Taipei, and plotting how they could one day reinstate themselves as the legitimate government of mainland China.

Meanwhile, the Kuomintang forces who had fled into Burma set about establishing a new base in the eastern province of Shan State. Their orders from Taipei were to continue to fight against Mao's forces over the border in Yunnan. At first, they were moderately successful, which was when they attracted the attention of the CIA.

America's ideological obsession with communism after World War II meant that it actively sought out allies who could help to contain its spread. When they saw the 'good work' that the Kuomintang was doing in China, the CIA were keen to help, so Washington facilitated the Kuomintang's ongoing armament with covert shipments flown in from the USA. For the next fifteen years, the US bankrolled the stateless rebels as they attempted to take back parts of China.

The problem was that several of the Kuomintang leaders were also getting rich off the local opium trade on the side, which should have put the CIA in a difficult position but Washington simply turned a blind eye to their allies' drug-related activities. Despite this being completely at odds with Washington's official anti-drug policies, the CIA's logic was that communist ideology was a far greater threat to the American people than heroin would ever be.

By the time America's involvement in the Vietnam War began in earnest in the early 1960s, the Kuomintang were the sole rulers of Shan and had turned the territory into the biggest opium production site in the world. Their revenue streams bloomed as their operations developed—all with the full support of US intelligence.

Now, even though we're talking about opium, it's important to consider the modus operandi of the Kuomintang because it shapes how the meth trade operates today. During the period of their alliance with the US, local villagers all over Shan State were coerced on pain of death into producing opium. Young men from villages were enlisted as mules to carry the drugs over the border to refineries in neighbouring Laos—a business model that would endure for decades to come.

But back on that day in 1967, in a 'sliding doors moment', everything could have been so different because the status quo was about to be challenged. The young upstart, Khun Sa, decided to forge his own path. Seeing how the Kuomintang generals were persecuting and exploiting the Shan people for their own benefit, he formed his own small militia and made a compelling counter-offer to local opium farmers.

The Shan people loved the tall, handsome and charismatic Khun Sa, and he loved them in return. He talked openly of building an army that could expel the invaders—the Kuomintang, the Americans, and even the Burmese who ruled Shan State from Rangoon. But for that he needed money, so he had gambled everything on getting one huge shipment of opium over the border to Laos, where his customer, Ouane Rattikone, a Lao army general who had aspirations to get into the global heroin business, would pay him a small fortune.

But the Kuomintang had other ideas. As soon as they heard of the caravan's existence, they realised that their fifteen-year monopoly over the Burmese opium trade was in danger of being fundamentally challenged and dispatched a battalion to stop Khun Sa before he could complete his deal.

On the night of 25 July, Khun Sa's smugglers parked their mules along the bank of the Mekong. His men sourced logs from a nearby lumberyard and created a high, semicircular barricade for protection while they waited for their customer to arrive. The Kuomintang forces caught up with them the following day, and the skirmish that followed made the news in Vientiane.

The news enraged General Ouane, who feared that the warring Burmese factions would bring too much heat to his covert heroin business. He ordered both sides to get out of Laos immediately—all deals were off. But the Kuomintang dismissed his request, scornfully demanding US$250,000 to leave, while Khun Sa ordered his men to maintain their position too, arguing that he had kept his side of the agreement and would only leave when he was paid in full.

More and more Kuomintang troops arrived over the next two days until the skirmish became a full-blown battle. Both sides were armed with an impressive array of weapons—machine guns, mortars and rifles. The noise could be heard for miles around.

General Ouane had had enough. He dispatched a squadron of T-28 fighter planes and scrambled a paratrooper battalion to move on the caravan. On the afternoon of 30 July, the sound of automatic weapons was suddenly drowned out by the roar of six T-28 prop fighters flying low up the Mekong river, followed by the deafening sound of 500-pound bombs crashing down indiscriminately on both Khun Sa and Kuomintang forces.

Under the pressure of the repeated bombing attacks, Khun Sa's men piled into boats and retreated across the Mekong. They abandoned not only the fallen bodies of eighty-two comrades but their opium as well. Meanwhile, the Kuomintang troops fled north along the Mekong, only to be cut off by the two Lao infantry battalions. With no other choice, they surrendered.

General Ouane Rattikone was the clear winner of what became known as the 1967 Opium War. He captured all of Khun Sa's raw opium, which he absorbed into his heroin business. Laos, an invaluable ally to the US war effort against the North Vietnamese, received no sanction from Washington, meaning the general was now free to become the number one producer of heroin in the world, all under the protection of the CIA.

His timing couldn't have been better. 'Number Four', the new injectable form of heroin the general began producing, was perfect for the battlefield. Light, cheap and moreish, Number Four created a sudden spike in heroin addiction among American GIs fighting over the border in Vietnam.

Ouane's refineries were staffed by skilled master chemists from Hong Kong and Taiwan who could produce high-grade heroin. Serious heroin addiction broke out in isolated units in the late 1960s and, by the end of the decade, the epidemic was fully developed. Ouane's heroin had become freely available at every US base from the Mekong Delta to the DMZ.

When US troops began withdrawing from Vietnam in 1971, the addicts were already returning home by the planeload, and the drugs were waiting for them when they arrived. Chinese, Corsican and American syndicates, who had already been exporting small quantities of heroin to the US, quickly expanded their operations, sending bulk shipments of Number Four to America to feed the demand.

By the end of 1971, the CIA's analysis of narcotics traffic in the Golden Triangle reported that the largest of Ouane's seven heroin factories, the same one that had once been the final destination of Khun Sa's opium, was producing more than 3 tonnes of heroin a year—the bulk of it for export to the USA. This was an enormous quantity, considering that American addicts were only estimated to be consuming a total of about 9 tonnes in total.

By 1975, the US faced a new war—the war on narcotics. The American people had to face up to the reality that supporting anti-communist governments in South-East

Asia had inadvertently created a market for heroin in their high schools.

Meanwhile, Khun Sa returned to Shan State and re-grouped. He emerged stronger, wiser and more determined than ever to succeed. As the Vietnam War ended, both the Kuomintang and General Ouane lost the support of their American backers in Washington. Khun Sa seized the opportunity to take control. Within a couple of years, he had established his own refineries, taking over the supply lines of his old enemies and establishing himself as the biggest heroin dealer in the world. By the end of the decade, he was single-handedly supplying more than a quarter of the world's heroin.

Could Khun Sa have achieved all that back in 1967? Almost certainly not. Arguably, the heroin trade between South-East Asia and the US needed the support of state-sized organisations like the Lao national army and the CIA to grow to the size it had. Khun Sa inherited a market that was exponentially more developed than the one he had tried to usurp eight years earlier.

But why have I chosen to tell you a story about heroin in the 1960s and '70s, when this book is about methamphetamine in the 2020s? The reason is that I see several parallels between the two stories that I think are important.

First, the CIA's involvement in South-East Asia in the mid-twentieth century set a dangerous precedent for the region. The idea that foreign powers could turn a blind eye to illegal activities in smaller states in the name of fighting a bigger cause is something that continues in Myanmar today. No longer is the US the superpower of influence in the region; now it is China who calls the shots in Asia.

Swap the CIA for China in the story and you can see the parallel today. Now China sees Myanmar as an important buffer state between it and the West. It would rather prop up a lawless backwater than open up a new frontier with the Western-leaning Indians and Thais. It suits China to indulge Myanmar's narco-state status, so it continues to allow the precursors for production to roll over the border from Chinese factories.

Second, the Kuomintang set the precedent for how politically motivated rebel militia groups could control regions within Myanmar. By coercing whole villages, they could enslave enough people to allow them to enter and dominate the narcotics trade. The men with the guns back then, just as the UWSA do today, could sustain their rebellions from the profits they made from drugs. It's not surprising that one group simply stepped into the shoes of the other.

Third, Khun Sa showed how individual upstarts could carve out niches for themselves in a crowded market. With enough chutzpah, there is no need to muscle in on the market when you can use your wiles to make money. Just as Zhao Wei does at Kings Romans today, there is room in the meth market for individuals to make themselves very rich by playing each side against the other and top-slicing the profits.

The most worrying parallel is the role of the state in the drug trade. The biggest army ultimately has the power to crush individual operatives and even sizeable militias. Today, the Myanmar Army, the Tatmadaw, has stepped into this role. Not to miss out on the billions of dollars being made, the Tatmadaw is the largest player in the meth trade. No matter how much money the UWSA or

Zhao Wei make, the Tatmadaw will always make more, just as Ouane did in his day.

A large part of that income today comes from cross-border drug flows. Just as happened in the 1960s, the person who controls the land earns money from taxing the flow of drugs that passes through it. Today rebel groups from the Akha, the Karen, the Wa, the Kachin and the Shan peoples, plus several other smaller ethnic armed militias, are taxing transactions in return for providing safe passage for meth through their spheres of influence. As long as the drugs keep moving south, there is money to be made indirectly from the trade.

Finally, the most depressing parallel of all is the seemingly endless flow of Western addicts creating the demand while Eastern regions produce the supply. There are more meth addicts per capita in Australia today than heroin addicts in the USA after the Vietnam War. The money being made from them is exponentially higher. The growth potential is even greater. It seems that whatever the high, wherever the person craving it is in the world, there is a corner of South-East Asia ready to produce and deliver it to your door.

The patterns of behaviour that were established over fifty years ago provided the foundations for the meth trade that we see today. Everything has changed but everything is the same.

————

Back in Tachileik, I follow Luke upstairs into a small strip-lit room where a TV plays cartoons in the corner. Luke invites me to sit on a rug in the middle of the floor as another man, who also looks Chinese, shuffles in. He's similar in age to Luke but he's wearing the traditional Burmese longyi, a kind of sarong, with a shawl tied around his neck. He reaches for the TV remote and kills the volume.

Michael introduces the new guy as Pho Tar, the first guy he met when he arrived in Tachileik. He says that they've been friends ever since and that I can trust him. I nod, even though I'm not sure I trust Michael yet, let alone his mate. Another guy—younger, wearing t-shirt and jeans, and covered in tattoos—comes in, scowling at me as he closes the door behind him. He says nothing as he sits down and lights a cigarette.

'He's Akha,' says Luke by way of explanation. The Akha are another minority ethnic group in Myanmar, currently fighting with the government in Yangon.

Michael squats on the floor, poised, maybe a little nervous at how the conversation is going to play out. I imagine that to Luke, I'm just another punter who Michael has brought here to score drugs. I can't see any reason to disabuse him of that view and so I ask him how much he can supply me. He shakes his head and explains that his boss was arrested in Laos recently and, like Bounsing's uncle, is facing the death penalty. The supply chain he used to control has now been taken over by a rival gang. Until things are resolved, he's out of the production business.

'I am not involved in production anymore but if you want something, I can bring it here.'

'Ice?' I ask.

He produces a bag of white crystals and throws it on the floor in front of me. This is the first time that I've seen crystal meth in Asia. I pick up the small plastic ziplock bag and examine it carefully. It's full of large white crystals that look like rock salt—around 10 grams of pure ice.

'Two thousand five hundred baht,' he says. Around US$75. One kilo would cost US$4000.

A kilo of this quality would easily fetch US$70,000 to $100,000 in Australia. Since I'd been in Australia, I'd wondered about the economics of the meth business. Newspaper reports often cite weights and measures of drug seizures and report on 'street value' but the figures often feel exaggerated, and dealers I've met call them unrealistic.

But the figures here are clear. A kilo of meth can be bought in Tachileik for US$4000 and, as I saw in Laos, smuggled over the border to Thailand for another US$4000. If you can get it from there to Sydney, then you can make up to twelve times what you paid for it. You can see why individuals get tempted into drug running. Especially if you were able to bump those quantities up to a commercial level and buy tonnes, not kilos—then the profits could be considerably more.

'I'm looking for more than this,' I tell Luke, surprised with how comfortable I've become with pretending to be a drug baron. 'A lot more. Kilograms. Multiple kilograms.'

'You need to speak with the people who run the machine,' Luke says.

Michael explains that 'the machine' is how they refer to the apparatus necessary to make synthetic drugs. Only the people who run the machine can discuss the kind of volume I've just mentioned.

There are different machines for different drugs in Asia. The machine that is used to produce ice is different from the one that's used to produce heroin or yaba. The presses for making pills are not illegal here, and you can buy them online from retail sites like Alibaba or Amazon for less than US$5000, including shipping.

Luke takes his phone out to show me a picture. It takes me a second to work out what I'm looking at. My eyes slowly focus and I realise the picture shows three sets of hands, reaching into a massive tray, counting out small pink pills into blue plastic bags. There are more pills than I can count. Tens and tens of thousands of them. Maybe as many as a million.

He nods as if to say, 'Yeah, that's right' and then scrolls to the next picture. This one shows ecstasy pills. There are Donald Trumps, UPS, Donkey Kongs—all labels and markings that you might see in a club in Europe or Australia. I had no idea Myanmar produced ecstasy too.

'It's a big factory, bigger than this building, with different spaces,' Luke says. 'In one space they do the mixing. Another they make the pills. They have an armed group there.'

Armed?

'Yes, of course,' he says. 'Rifles. This is the deep jungle. It is very dangerous.'

Luke passes me another bag containing a dozen small, pink-coloured pills. I shake one out onto the palm of my hand, noting the 'WY' logo stamped onto it. This is yaba.

'Listen,' he says, his eyes now pin-sharp, locked on to mine, 'if you want to talk to the people who run the machine, then you need to go to Mong Hsat.'

He opens his phone and pulls up a local map. He lays it on the table and sketches a line with his finger running west from Tachileik. Eventually, he stops on a small town called Mung Yung.

'This place,' he says. 'It is the top place where they produce in Myanmar. There is the machine. You can see it. You can talk with them.'

Michael nods in agreement. 'Yes. It's true,' he says. 'But be careful because if you work with these too long, you cannot leave anymore. They will kill you before they let you leave. These guys are the real mafia.'

'I only tell you this because I know him,' Luke says, pointing at Michael. 'If you go somewhere else, you are in danger. This is mafia. Don't go to someone else, don't ask anyone else about this business.'

Are we talking about UWSA? The Wa?

'I don't want to talk about that now,' he says. 'This is their main business but I can't talk about it. You get that, right?'

The civil war that rages in Myanmar today does so in different areas of the country. The eastern part of the country is divided along ethnic lines and several of the ethnic groups, seeking autonomy from the government in Yangon, have taken up arms: the Karen, the Kachin, the Kokang, the Shan and the largest force of all—the Wa.

The Wa are by far the largest army, estimated to have as many as 40,000 troops. For forty years they have been the fiercest opponents of the government. Wa territory is considered a no-go zone to both Burmese and foreigners. It's been said that it's easier to get into North Korea than Wa. Mong Hsat, the town that Luke is proposing I visit, is situated along the frontline of the hostilities between the Wa and the Myanmar Army.

How can I go to Mong Hsat? That whole area is closed to foreigners.

Luke waves away my question like he's waving off a fly.

'I can get the permit, and I'm an American.'

What? I don't know which of those statements surprises me more.

'Yeah, man, I lived in Phoenix and then in Iowa. I worked two years in the US. You don't believe me? Here's my passport.'

He holds out a passport with a familiar blue cover and the distinctive eagle crest under which I can read the words 'United States of America'. He opens it out to show me his mugshot inside. The guy who's going to show me the Wa's meth lab is a US citizen.

'Yeah, man,' he says. 'My mom is Karen. My dad is Chinese. But I'm an American citizen.'

I'm stunned. Luke explains to me that he was sent to study at Arizona State University ten years ago by the people he now works for. Before I can ask why, he moves on.

'I can get you into Mong Hsat but then you will need to walk for a few hours in the jungle. That okay?' he asks.

Sure. I'm happy.

'Okay, man, so you gonna go to Mong Hsat. Are you ready?'

Any time.

'This is a very dangerous job,' Michael pitches in. His expression is pinched, his eyes shifty and concerned.

'Yes,' Luke agrees. 'Because the machine you will see is very close to Thai border. Controlled by the ethnic armed group, but you don't have to worry about security. They are going to take care of it.'

I still can't believe that Luke is offering to get me access to one of the largest meth-production facilities in the country, where I can see how they mix the ingredients, as well as how they press and package it for export.

'This is a big one, man,' he says. 'This one I chose because it is safe. But no cameras or phones, okay? If they find a device on you then you're going to have a problem.'

I'm not likely to do anything that causes a problem with a gang of meth-exporting gangsters in the jungle but at the same time I'm gagging to see inside the factory he's describing to me.

The Akha guy goes off to get beers for everyone. We crack them open and the conversation carries on between the others in Burmese for a little while. I secretly record some of their conversation on my phone and later play it to my friend who speaks fluent Burmese. I'm worried in case they're planning to double-cross me but my friend reassures me that they were only discussing the logistics of the trip.

That night, I'm preoccupied with thoughts of what is happening out in the jungle, where law and order are no longer under the control of the government. Out there is rebel country, where ethnic armed groups fight to hang on to the land they've secured through decades of war. I feel exhilarated at the idea that I might be the first outsider to see parts of that territory. That I might even be inside a meth lab. I will get primary evidence that at least one of the major armed groups inside Myanmar is directly involved in the meth trade, something they have all denied.

When Michael drops me at my hotel the next morning, he looks stressed.

'What's wrong? I thought that went well.'

'Don't trust your knee,' he says.

Don't trust your *knee*? What does that mean?

Michael swings his leg over the seat of his bike and plants his foot firmly onto the dirt where we're standing. He reaches out and puts his hand on his knee.

'This is my own knee and I can't even trust it,' he says. 'If I cannot trust my knee, how can I trust anybody?'

While I consider this metaphor and what it might mean, Michael kickstarts his wife's motorcycle and takes off.

———

Back in my room, I make a call to the head of the Australian Federal Police in Asia, Glen McEwen. Glen's based out of Beijing and has been in-post for nearly three years. Most of Australia's anti-drug-smuggling efforts are coordinated by the AFP, who have bureaus across Asia staffed by the same agents I spoke to in chapter two. To give you a sense of how important the Australian government consider this post, Glen controls 37 per cent of the whole Australian national anti-drug budget. His network stretches across eleven locations—Beijing, Guangzhou, Hong Kong, Hanoi, Ho Chi Minh City, Phnom Penh, Bangkok, Yangon, Colombo, New Delhi and Islamabad.

Despite that, Glen says that it's impossible to be 100 per cent sure about much when it comes to the connection between Australian meth and the drugs being produced in Myanmar.

'The problem is I can't access these areas myself,' Glen tells me. 'We're completely reliant on intel that comes out of the country to us.'

The AFP have officially been 'based' in Myanmar for twelve years but Glen says none of his operatives ever leave Yangon. I've encountered situations like this before, where the security risk to foreign experts visiting the areas where drugs are being produced is too high, so they remain entirely reliant on third-party intel. I once stood in an Afghan poppy field talking on the phone to the head of the local UNODC bureau, who confessed to me that he had never actually seen a poppy.

Since I've been in Myanmar, people keep asking me why it's so important to go and see things for myself. The answer is because guys like Glen don't. I've read hundreds of pages of reports and academic papers on methamphetamine but I find reading something written by someone who hasn't seen it for themselves unsatisfying. I've been lied to a hundred times since I got here and I'm not taking anyone's version of anything as the truth anymore. I want to see for myself. I want you to read this and know that I'm not giving you a secondhand account of anything.

For example, one of the recent reports produced by the UNODC claims that most methamphetamine coming out of Myanmar now is from so-called 'super-labs' created by people from outside of Myanmar, cooked by people who aren't from Myanmar. Their best guess is that mafia groups are renting territory from ethnic armed groups and militias inside of Myanmar and running a sort of rental and protection arrangement. It's entirely possible, likely even, but where is the evidence coming from?

There's a problem with relying too heavily on the testimony of others when producing reports. Another recent report produced by the UN on opium production outlined areas where it claimed that an armed ethnic Kachin group from the north of the country, the KIO, were growing poppies. The problem was that area was controlled by the Myanmar Army and not the KIO. The KIO produced a very robust and embarrassing rebuttal soon after the UN report was published.

You might wonder how the United Nations could get something like that so wrong. Like much in Myanmar, the answer lies in politics. As with the AFP, the UN have to rely on secondhand information. And guess who provided them with the information on the KIO poppy fields? The Myanmar Army. So they got played. The UNODC got played. They put out a report that wrongly blamed one party for something they weren't doing and turned something that could have been used to bring people around the table for a discussion into something that did the opposite. It completely backfired.

I can't help but feel that this is all down to the same shortcomings around security that Glen described to me; if you want to know the truth about something then you have to go and find out for yourself. In a situation where so many interested parties have such divergent vested interests, how can you rely on the information that they are providing you as being balanced and fair? You can't.

I'm going to find out as much as I can find out about the Meth Road myself and I can't do that without going out there and getting into areas like Wa State—places that the experts are not allowed to access. Tomorrow, that means that I am going to have to trust my knee. I'm going to trust it to take me to Wa.

6

WELCOME TO WA

The road to Mong Hsat is horrible and I've been on some bad roads in my day. Every second there's a pothole bigger than the last, so it's impossible to take my eyes off the road at all. My body is constantly braced for the next time the car bounces, protecting my head from bouncing off the roof.

Along the way, Luke fills me in on his background. I'm keen to understand why someone with a US passport chooses instead to live in Tachileik. He says that his main business is running gaming machines, like the one I saw in his shop. He has several more around town—one in every casino.

'They do good business,' he says, 'so I have cash to invest.'

A few years ago, it occurred to Luke that he could multiply his earnings from the gaming machines by pumping the money back into meth labs, which promised him a quick return on his investment. He says that now he is a 'minor shareholder' in several facilities dotted all over Shan State. He owns 30 per cent of the lab he's arranged for me to see.

'Last year, if you'd come here, they would say "no" for sure,' he says, 'but this year business is not so good. There are too many people doing this business now, so if they don't get an order, they cannot earn money.'

And what about the American passport?

That was arranged for him by his 'big boss'. Luke was sent to the US to see if there was a way to move into the lucrative meth market there. That explains why he was living in places like Iowa and Arizona—areas with well-documented high addiction rates. It didn't go to plan. He says the power of the Mexican cartel was too strong.

'The US is still a market for Mexico,' he says, 'but I think it will change. What about the UK? Is there really a chance for business there?'

I realise that he's being serious and suddenly understand why he's taking me to see his lab. He's working the angle in case I could be a route to a new market. I decide that it's not in my interest to disappoint him, so I reply, 'Maybe, let's see.'

'You're going to Mong Hsat to see the priest there, okay?'

A plausible cover story. So we're missionaries?

'Yeah, Christian missionaries,' he laughs.

After three hours, we pass an army checkpoint where there's a soldier stationed at the barrier. He barely moves as we pass by. I notice on the top of the hill a heavily fortified military position, watchtowers, surrounded by concentric circles of spiked fencing and razor wire. We've entered a militarised area.

Where are we?

'This area is Wa,' says Pho Tar. 'The UWSA control all this.'

From the look of the fortifications around us, I'd say the United Wa State Army, the official arm of the Wa, and the largest armed group in the country other than the national army, looks like a very modern military outfit, but its reputation goes back to colonial times.

The original Wa territory consists of the jungles between the two main thoroughfares of north-east Myanmar that lie directly along the Chinese border: Muse to the north and Mong La to the south. Traders have always been able to give it a wide berth. There's never been a reason to go to Wa unless you really had to.

Wa has always been considered to be the least accessible part of Myanmar and, in fact, one of the least accessible areas in the world. For centuries these lands were considered off-limits to foreigners unless you brought your army with you and were ready to use it.

The Wa are a largely pastoral people with their own language and culture, farming the highlands either side of the Myanmar–China border for the last 200 years. The Wa can legitimately claim to be indigenous to the region.

For a long time, the Wa had a bit of a reputation. According to Wa mythology, the north-west region they control is the spring from which all human existence emerged and so, as the custodians of those sacred lands, with a duty to keep their gods sweet, the Wa engaged in human sacrifice, slaughtering and eating their enemies, and using their skulls to line the pathways to their villages.

The British referred to the Wa as the Wild Wa after two British soldiers lost their heads during a surveying trip in 1898. Their early demise meant that the precise limits of Wa territory remained unclear, adding to the mystery of what lay within.

At a time when the rest of the world seemed to be getting smaller, Wa remained an undefined region of barbarian headhunters, residing in impenetrable jungle lands, growing illegal crops and fuelling the international drug market. The rumours were enough to keep people away, and the truth of what went on inside Wa territory remained elusive, fuelling the imaginations of those who wondered about it further. Other than a few opium and salt traders, nobody else dared to visit, and so nobody wrote much more about the Wa—and what was written was largely copied from what had previously been written.

As so often happens, gaps in knowledge were filled with the worst imaginable horrors, and the reputation of the Wa as flesh-eating monsters endured right into the middle of the twentieth century. Until I'd heard the story of Michael's father, I'd imagined these takes to be apocryphal but now I'm not so sure.

Modern events haven't exactly helped to uncover the truth about what was going on inside Wa either. After the Burmese government was toppled by the military coup in 1962, the army began a massive counterinsurgency campaign, using the 'Four Cuts' strategy, intended to suppress support for the Wa from ethnic communities by cutting off their food, funds, intelligence and recruits.

The Burmese military began attacking and destroying villages, killing or torturing anyone suspected of aiding any opposition groups. Entire communities were forced to move out of their areas and anyone trying to remain in their homes was shot on sight.

Some groups surrendered and signed the ceasefire with the government, agreeing to come over to join the state's struggle against their enemies. Others entrenched their positions, strengthening their armies and increasing the intensity of their struggle against the national army. The largest of these was the UWSA.

Today, other than one authorised PR junket for the world's press to take a carefully stage-managed tour of the capital, Pangkham, in 2018, nobody who isn't Wa or Chinese ever visits the northern Wa State.

The territory we have passed into, on the way to Mong Hsat, is what is known as the southern region of Wa State or 'Southern Wa', separated from the northern state by hundreds of kilometres. Twenty-five years ago, in return for helping the government to finally defeat the drug lord Khun Sa, the Wa were rewarded with a patch of land stretching along the southern Thai border. These lands are much flatter and more fertile than the mountainous terrain of the north but the problem was that there weren't any Wa people living here to work them.

So the UWSA decided to populate the Southern Wa region with its people from the north. Certain villages and towns were earmarked for repatriation, and the orders were sent out that the people living there would make the 2000-kilometre journey south.

Back on the road to Mong Hsat, a few kilometres from the Wa checkpoint we enter a small town where Pho Tar says we will stop for a few minutes. This is too good an opportunity to pass up. I have somehow, by mistake, with a permit to visit Mong Hsat, passed into Wa territory, so I decide to take a walk into the centre of the town.

The town is really a couple of roughly cobbled streets, with a general store at one end and the distant mountains, where the sun is beginning to set, at the other. There are few cars, the locals preferring to get around on cheap Chinese mopeds. A woman in a bright-red headscarf with a baby thrown over her shoulder passes me, staring in such a way as to suggest that she hasn't seen many people like me before.

I spot a house where a bunch of people are sitting on the porch outside. An old woman, who I guess is in her seventies, eyes me suspiciously. Her skin is dark and deeply lined but she still has a thick head of grey hair, tied up in a pink bandana. In her arms, a tiny baby is sleeping. Her expression remains fixed as I approach and say hello.

The moment of awkwardness is broken when two teenagers look up from a moped they seem to be repairing. One of the boys explains that this is his family house, they are Wa, and the old lady is his grandmother. She came here with the boy's mother twenty years ago. When I introduce myself, they seem as interested in me as I am in them.

'I was born in Wa,' the old lady eventually explains, meaning the northern Wa State. 'I lived there for my whole life but then they came to tell us we could not stay anymore. They came into the village and we could only take what we could carry. I carried my baby.'

She was loaded onto a truck along with other women and small children and driven south across Shan State. Many others, mostly men, were told to walk. The journey took months, hard walking through the densest jungles; tens of thousands died along the way from malaria and dengue fever.

When the forced migration was finished, there were as many as 100,000 Wa people freshly arrived in Southern Wa, ready to begin work. The Lahu and Akha people living there were thrown off the land and many were pushed over the border to refugee camps in Thailand. The message was clear—this is Wa territory now and you're no longer welcome.

I'm struck by the simplicity of life here in Wa. There are no signs of ruthless organised criminals, no obvious drug use and certainly no paths lined with human skulls. This seems to me an agrarian community, quietly going about its business. The only sign that this is not some bucolic idyll is the sight of a passing soldier on a motor-cycle now and again.

'When I am sixteen, I will join the army,' says one of the boys. 'But my brother will not have to join. He will go to study in Thailand.'

The rules in Wa state that every family must give one son to the army to fight the good fight. There's no arguing; it's a Wa family's duty and they do it without question. This is how they have achieved their status in Myanmar and why they have maintained their political influence for so long.

Pho Tar comes to find me, keen that we get back on the road as it's already getting dark. Reluctantly, I say goodbye to the Wa family and return to the car. We leave the village and continue the drive towards Mong Hsat.

We soon pass another fortified hill and another checkpoint. The sun goes down across the paddy fields, lighting the sky red and gold. I can't help but wonder if the real point of this displaced population is to supply soldiers for the UWSA, who keep the area off-limits so that the drug lords can operate their meth business without outside interference.

An hour later, we reach the checkpoint outside of Mong Hsat, and Pho Tar gets out and speaks to the soldiers. One of them comes to the window and shines his torch inside the car to take a good look at me. He talks again briefly to Pho Tar and a couple of minutes later we are through the barrier, driving into town. Tonight we will sleep and tomorrow we will leave the vehicle and make the journey south on foot, into the deep jungle, where we will see the lab.

———

I'm up early enough to take a stroll around Mong Hsat without drawing attention to myself. The streets are empty save for the odd early bird and the sun has yet to rise high enough to heat the day. I realise that I'm feeling cold for the first time in weeks.

The street from my hotel leads directly from the airport towards the main 'downtown' area. Across the street, there's a huge two-storey mansion of palatial proportions, surrounded by a 3-metre fence topped with limb-slicing razor wire. Next to it is another mansion and then another and another. This is the Vaucluse of Asia.

Beyond this street, the rest of town is basic and the houses are single-storey concrete or wooden shacks. The main drag is comprised of a row of tea shops and noodle stalls and there's a pool hall with a single snooker table for those who want to let their hair down. How on earth do the people who live here afford such massive houses?

As the town begins to come to life, I'm aware of more motorcycles buzzing around. One local woman does a double-take as she passes by, which makes me a bit self-conscious. It's time for me to get off the street. I don't want the rumour going around town that there's an outsider in town so I hurry back to meet Pho Tar and the tattooed Akha guy. They're waiting for me and they aren't happy.

Tattoo guy passes me his phone to show me a picture shot from the upstairs floor of the place we bedded down last night. It shows a single figure slouched in the seat next to where we're now standing. I look more closely and see it was taken at 5.15 a.m.

'Secret police,' says Pho Tar. Tattoo guy shakes his head with displeasure.

We're being followed. The guys think that as soon as we crossed the checkpoint last night, a red flag was raised. It's now vital, they say, that I go on acting like a Christian missionary so that hopefully our tail will get bored and leave us alone. We will go into town, act normal, buy some stuff in the market and pay a visit to the church. The trip to the lab will have to wait.

I wish I could say that seeing the sights of Mong Hsat was a fun and rewarding experience but after you've seen the church, the market and the snooker table, there isn't much else. Every time I look up, the secret police are there, following behind, watching my every move. For another two days, I play along until eventually Pho Tar says that it's safe; the cops are happy that I'm not up to any skulduggery.

That afternoon, tattoo guy, Pho Tar and I head out of town towards the lab. I'm finally on my way to see the elusive machine, what feels to me like the Holy Grail. Soon I'm going to see what no Westerner has ever seen before. This is it.

Tattoo guy insists that I hand over my phone. He takes the SIM card out of it so that the GPS will no longer register my location and places both inside the glove box. He says I can have them back when we return from the jungle.

The lab is a three-hour drive from town and then a two-hour walk through the jungle, so we'll have to walk in the dark but Pho Tar explains that won't matter as the lab is operational twenty-four hours a day. Then he asks, ever so politely, if he can cover my eyes. I agree and he blindfolds me with a t-shirt. I'm amused that he thinks I would ever have the slightest chance of retracing our steps.

Behind my blindfold, it occurs to me that I'm driving into the jungle flanked by a pair of Chinese gangsters to see their meth lab, phone-less and with no plan B if things get hairy. I'm entirely at the mercy of two guys I met only days ago, blindly hoping that all this will be worthwhile and I will get to see the elusive machine.

138

I listen to the two men talking animatedly in the car and begin to get an anxious feeling that something is going wrong. Pho Tar pulls the t-shirt off my head and, as my eyes adjust once more to the light, he shakes his head and points to the rear window of the vehicle. We have a tail. The secret police are following us again. Tattoo guy turns the car around and we head back to the hotel. I'm deflated, frustrated and not entirely missing the irony that the reason I can't see a meth lab is not because the gangsters that run it don't want me to but because the police don't.

That evening, Luke calls to say that he has spoken with the head of the police in Tachileik to explain the situation. This strikes me as strange. In return for a bribe, the police chief has called off his men and suggested to Luke that there is a way for me to see the lab without anyone losing face—we get up at 4 a.m., leave town via the official checkpoint and then double back along a track that tattoo guy knows, which leads back to the lab. It's a longer walk for us to take but means that the secret police will leave us alone. Happy that we're back on, I agree and set my alarm.

It's 4.30 a.m. and I'm standing in the lobby of the hotel waiting for Pho Tar and tattoo guy, ready and pumped to go again. Pho Tar appears at the top of the stairs, gabbling into his phone, so I motion to him that we need to get going. The sun will be up in an hour and everyone was keen last night that we'd leave in darkness. Pho Tar hands the phone to me. It's Luke.

'We have a problem,' he says.

What now? I'm sick of hearing about problems. I just want to get going.

'The Akha guy with the tattoos, you know?' he says.

Yeah, of course, I know him. Where is he?

'He is running,' says Luke. 'He took two guns, four thousand dollars of my money and my car.'

Pho Tar looks crestfallen. He knows that they have lost face and he looks genuinely pissed off about it. His mate slipped out in the middle of the night, stole his gun (I didn't realise he was carrying one until then), jumped in Luke's four-wheel drive and drove off into the night.

Now Luke wants me to come back to Tachileik.

'I can't find someone else to take you now,' he says. 'I have to find him. This isn't going to end well for him, you know?'

I suggest we find someone else. I suggest we find the 'secret road' ourselves. I suggest that I wait here as long as it takes to find a tattoo guy replacement. Luke won't hear any other ideas. His only priority is to find his man. I'm so disappointed I almost offer to kill him myself.

I have no choice but to return to Tachileik empty-handed.

———

Two weeks later, Luke is back in touch. This time he wants me to fly from Tachileik to the Shan capital, Taunggyi, to meet another of his contacts. Even though this is the call that I've been waiting for, hassling him for news almost daily, I'm starting to feel as though the search for more details about meth production here is a fruitless one. I tell Luke that I will go but that I want to take Michael with me, so the next day, we jump on a plane to make the thirty-minute flight north.

I'm exhausted from months of travelling, even more so from the months of negotiating and disappointment. Every attempt to either meet a meth cook or see a lab for myself has been thwarted by secret police or an army checkpoint or someone running off with Luke's vehicle and all his money. Nonetheless, I'm trying to remain optimistic, telling myself that having Michael with me might make the difference.

At the airport, we take a cab into town and meet with Luke's contact in Taunggyi. The man is older, early fifties, his demeanour more serious and mature than anyone else I've met in Myanmar. He nods silently while Michael translates and I explain what I've come to see. Eventually, he takes out his phone and hands it to me.

'Hello?' I say.

'Hello,' a voice replies in English. 'He says you can go with him now. But he must take your phone and when you reach the jungle, he must cover your head. It's okay?'

I'm almost getting used to this.

The next morning we're off in a four-wheel drive again. We take the road east for four hours before we turn south, heading into the jungle again. Sitting next to me, Michael is unusually quiet. After a while, they blindfold us both which makes the journey feel rougher as the LandCruiser jerks and jolts over potholes that feel like the size of swimming pools. Maybe he's anxious, I think. It's funny how I've grown to know Michael so well that I can now interpret his moods. A few hours later, I calculate that we could be 80 kilometres or more south of the road from Taunggyi, which would put us deep into Wa territory again, only this time coming from the north.

We must have passed through checkpoints along the way, where ordinarily I would have been asked to hand over my passport, maybe even get out of the car so that a soldier could inspect me, but we haven't stopped once. We must have just sailed through unmolested, meaning that someone with influence has smoothed our way.

I hear the man we met in Taunggyi issuing an instruction before Michael takes off my blindfold. When my eyes adjust, all I can see is dense forest on both sides and a dark-red track out in front of us. Michael starts chirruping in Burmese to the man in the front seat, who grunts and harrumphs a couple of replies. Michael translates for me. We are close to our destination, and from there we must walk because there is no more road. He says that someone will meet us who knows the way.

Twenty minutes later, the vehicle stops where I can see a group of people sitting around a makeshift camp: a tarpaulin thrown up between a couple of trees, a metal pot hanging over a smoking fire. Half a dozen tired-looking people gaze over in our direction, their faces an odd mix of curiosity and removal.

At once, a much larger man emerges from beneath the tarp and approaches the car, wiping his hands on his trousers and talking fast. The Taunggyi man steps out of the car and they seem to argue for a couple of minutes. Michael shakes his head at me when I suggest we get out. 'Wait,' he says.

Eventually the Taunggyi man opens the door on Michael's side and ushers him out. Yet again, I'm frustrated at how little I can glean without knowing any of the language, but the larger man seems to be shouting at Michael. Soon, the three of them are locked in a very animated debate.

I have a curious thought that I should feel frightened, at least anxious about where I am and what is happening. These men are criminals—gangsters, no less—and we are who knows where, in the middle of the jungle in the middle of disputed territory during an active conflict. If these guys wanted to, they could shoot us and bury our bodies in the jungle where nobody would ever find us. And yet, I feel numb to any fear. I feel irritated that they're arguing again, bored of the constant conflict that occurs every single time we try to do anything in this godforsaken place, tired of nothing ever being straightforward. Getting shot in the head now might almost offer some relief from it all.

Michael returns to the car and informs me (yet again) that the plan has changed. The large man says that no way can I go to the lab, that my white skin will draw too much attention. What he is prepared to do is allow Michael to go and make a video of what they are doing there. But there is another condition—the video must be shot on his own phone, and I can only watch the video when they return. After that, the phone and the video must remain in the jungle.

With a sigh, I agree. There is nothing more to be done as I have zero leverage. I have to accept that I'll never actually see inside a Burmese jungle meth lab but what I might get to see is what happens inside of one. Sometimes you just have to accept that this is as good as it gets. A video should at least help me to answer the big questions I have about the method of production that these guys are using and at what scale they are operating.

Then the local man reveals that he has still one more condition. I watch as he makes Michael strip naked in the clearing, meticulously going through his clothing, confiscating his phone and checking for any secret recording devices. Michael's skinny body looks so vulnerable and his face is contorted in disgust. I can tell this is humiliating for him.

'Are you okay, Michael?' I ask.

'I am scared,' he replies. 'You must promise me, if I do not come back, you will take care of my family.'

I think of Michael's two young children. For a moment, I consider telling him to forget it, take back his clothes and get into the car. If we leave now, we can be back in Taunggyi by nightfall. We can drink some beers and laugh at how crazy we were to ever have considered this a good idea.

But we both know that is no longer an option.

'Okay, Michael, I'll see you in a couple of hours' is all I can say.

The large man, the man from Taunggyi and a couple of the others who have been standing around, watching events unfold, disappear into the forest with Michael. Nobody who remains in the camp speaks to me; nobody even comes near me. I sit back in the car and wait. Whatever happens, I know that this is the end of my time in Myanmar. It is time to leave. I've been here long enough to understand what is happening, but I also have to understand that I will never know it all, never see everything. I will accept whatever Michael returns with as the best I'm going to get here and move on with my story.

I need the toilet so I find a corner of the camp, a little away from the fire, where I spot a pile of discarded sacks, plastic barrels and blue oil drums. Next to them is the burned-out remains of a large bonfire. I assume that this is where the cooks have been burning their waste.

Most of the bottles are only labelled in Chinese, but some of the sacks and drums have both Chinese and Western chemical symbols. My high school chemistry is a little rusty but I recognise the symbols for sodium cyanide and hydrochloric acid, lime and sodium hydroxide pellets. I shudder at the thought of what these noxious chemicals might be doing to the surrounding environment.

The bottles offer some clues as to how these guys are making meth. If you have sodium cyanide, then it's a two-step method to make one of the main precursors needed to make meth—phenyl-2-propanone, or P2P. First you mix the sodium cyanide with benzyl chloride to make benzyl cyanide. P2P is easily made from that.

I'm a little surprised. This is not a method that has been reported much in this part of the world until very recently. The UNODC reported that in 2020, record seizures of sodium cyanide, amounting to almost 108 tonnes, were reported by Myanmar, compared with the 4.6 tonnes reported in 2019. Benzyl cyanide has been regulated in China as a Class III drug precursor since June 2021, making it a lot harder to buy openly, but benzyl chloride isn't a scheduled chemical so it's easier to get hold of.

Reporting on recent seizures in 2020, the UNODC found that around 100 litres of P2P was discovered in Myanmar and another 2800 litres in China, mostly from illicit laboratories or warehouses, indicating that it had been illegally manufactured rather than diverted from a legitimate source. It's possible that some of the Chinese seizures were bound for Myanmar but nobody is sure. Comparing this to Mexico, where 11,000 litres of P2P was seized in the same year, it's unclear whether P2P meth is on the rise in Myanmar, but discovering the precursors to make P2P in the trash could be an important piece of the jigsaw puzzle. If that is the case, then the authorities may need to devise appropriate approaches to stem the flow of these precursors.

You may have read scare stories in the press that P2P meth is more dangerous than ephedrine-produced meth but they are just different pathways to the same drug. There is no scientific evidence supporting the idea that P2P-produced meth is any more or less neurotoxic than ephedrine meth but what these clues do suggest to me is that someone here is producing at volume and quantity. Chris and the shake-and-bake crew aren't making P2P meth, and what they make is not particularly pure. But these guys in the jungle clearly are making P2P meth, which means it's stronger than anything coming out of Chris's kitchen and therefore likely to have stronger effects when you inject an equivalent amount into your veins.

———

Four hours later, the sun is lower in the sky and the mosquitos are biting. Some of the guys around the camp have fallen asleep and I'm worried that if Michael doesn't return soon, I'm going to have to sleep in the car.

But then, an hour after sundown, Michael returns, stumbling into the camp behind the Taunggyi man and the larger man. His face looks drawn, worn down perhaps by the stress of the situation, probably wondering if he would ever make it back here. He nods sadly to me as he enters the clearing and collects a water bottle from the car. I can see beads of sweat on his forehead and his clothes look damp. It seems like wherever the lab was, it was quite a trek from here.

'Did you see everything?' I ask.

'I saw everything,' Michael replies, downing the water in one go. 'The den where they are working is far from here, in the jungle.'

The large man hands me his phone. He has opened a video, which he invites me to play. I move back to the car, setting the screen down on the dashboard so that I can watch and hear everything before I hit play.

I immediately see the back of Michael's head in the video. The footage seems to have been recorded by the large man as he follows Michael through dense forest, into a clearing, where a group of local Burmese people are busy working. Everyone looks up briefly, noticing the phone, curious as to why the boss has turned up with a stranger perhaps. I'm surprised to see their faces, having assumed that they would be wearing masks to protect themselves from breathing in noxious chemicals.

There's a loud buzzing noise, maybe the sound of a generator somewhere, but I can still hear the large man speaking to one of the men in the group. Michael, never short of something to say, begins chiming in, and an animated discussion follows, off-camera, which I don't even try to understand. I'm more interested in watching the action.

The large man continues walking around and the camerawork is distinctly unsteady as he moves past the people, past a pile of blue plastic drums, which look the same as the ones I saw in the camp. Finally he reaches a tarpaulin that looks like it's been tied between the trees, forming a sort of awning against a rocky overhang that leads into a shallow cave.

'That is the den,' Michael says. I hadn't heard him get into the seat behind me but now he's watching the video over my shoulder. 'Now you can see the machine.'

I asked Michael to make sure he described as much as possible while he was at the jungle lab. He's clearly misunderstood because on the video, I can hear him saying, 'Right now the man is making a video of the den where they make the ice.'

At the entrance to the den, I can see more blue plastic drums and sacks of chemicals stacked to one side of the room. There are a dozen people moving around, getting in the way of the shot. Two men hold a sack over a large metal container while a woman uses a tool to scoop out kilograms of white powder.

'This is the chemical for making the ice,' Michael says helpfully.

'What chemical is it?' I ask.

A conversation between Michael and the large man ensues. It seems like Michael doesn't understand what the man is saying. Or maybe he doesn't know how to translate it.

'Can he write it down?' I ask. Michael translates my question and the large man calls me out of the car and shuts the door.

He squats down and licks his finger. With his wet digit, he traces out the chemical formula in the dirt on the car door—$C_6H_5CH_2COCH_3$. I instantly recognise this as the formula for phenyl-2-propanone or P2P.

This is the confirmation I wanted. The rubbish that I'd seen on the bonfire earlier fits with this method of production. The large man and his team are not using a pseudoephedrine-reduction route to make meth but are employing a more sophisticated, higher-yielding P2P pathway that requires more technical know-how and explains why the equipment in the video isn't what I was expecting.

I return my attention to the video where, in the centre of the den, I can see what Michael has been talking about all this time—the machine. The machine is industrial. The image that I'd always had in my head was that it would look like a bigger version of a school chemistry lab, but what I'm looking at is entirely different. As the large man scans the camera around the inside of the den, I can see that there are no glass bottles, no glass condensers, no plastic tubing or round-bottomed flasks. This is entirely more sophisticated than I'd imagined.

The lab has been set up by someone who knows what they're doing and who has spent a lot of cash doing it. This is not a shake-and-bake set up. This is not even a scaled-up version of Dale Francis Drake's lab in Gympie. It's something way more professional.

First, there is a large, shiny metal tank, like a hot-water tank that you might see in a laundry cupboard. It's hard to be sure but I'd guess it holds around 200 litres. The wall of the tank is covered in red Chinese symbols and has several metal valves sticking out of it. Running from the top is a long metal tube, like an air-conditioning pipe, which runs horizontally and then connects at the top of another metal tank, smaller, roughly a third of the size of the big tank, and shaped like an egg. This I recognise as a batch reactor.

Batch reactors are used in industrial chemical plants to mix the precursors needed for large production runs. The advantage of the batch reactor is that it guarantees a controlled environment for your reaction. You simply pour the chemicals into the reactor, which contains an agitator to do the stirring, while an internal cooling system maintains the chemicals at a constant temperature and pressure. There's no need for you to touch the mixture. You can just let it run for the required time, and then, when you're ready, you run off the finished product from a tap at the bottom. Batch reactors mean that the whole process remains sealed, reducing the risk of being exposed to poisonous chemicals. You can pick one up in China for around US$5000.

'How much can this one produce?' I ask the large man. Michael translates.

He explains that the machine works to order. When a customer makes a request, they fire it up and begin production, working nonstop in shifts until the order is filled. To work in the den, each villager must make a commitment to remain for one year. Nobody is allowed to leave during that time except when they are given special leave to visit their families.

'Then they are allowed to go out and see their relative or their parents,' Michael explains. 'But they cannot talk about anything, and if they run from the job, then their family will not be safe anymore.'

The large man says that a typical order from a customer is usually between 50 and 200 kilograms. The machine

A checkpoint along the Myanmar–Thai border.

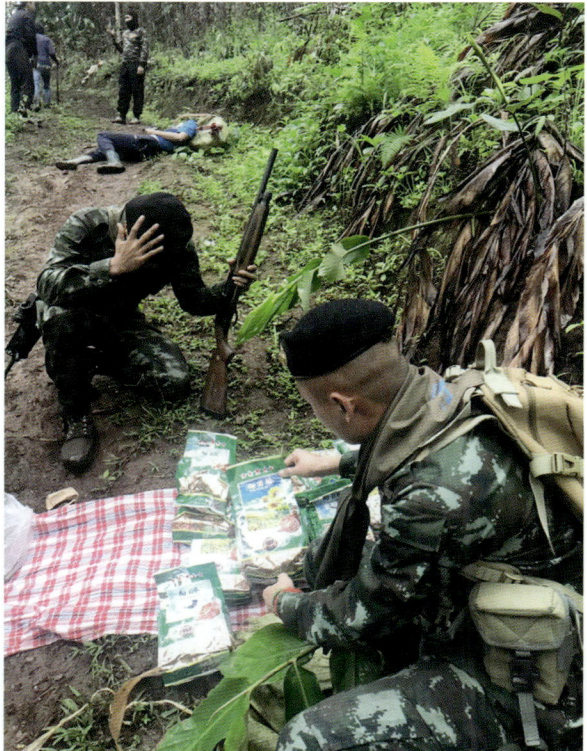

The Thai Phamuang military anti-drugs taskforce discovers ice smuggled in green tea packets. A smuggler's corpse lies in the background.

Homemade backpacks are used to smuggle kilograms of ice over the Myanmar–Thai border.

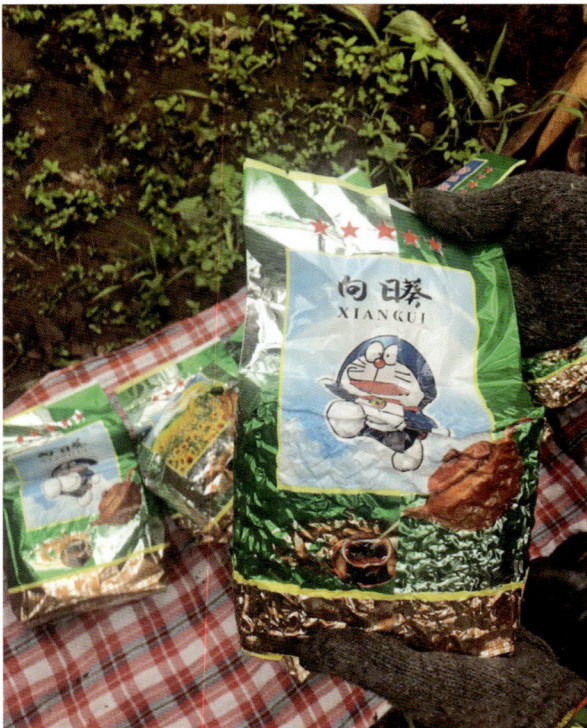

Producers use brands of green tea to identify their supplies.

Thai DEA celebrating a bust.

Surveillance cameras
cover every inch
of the Mekong in
the Golden Triangle.

The golden dome of Kings Romans casino and its hotel behind it.

Kings Romans casino floor.

The only Rolls-Royce in Kings Romans: Zhao Wei's.

A tiger caged in a park near Kings Romans, destined for human consumption.

Michael and me, partners in crime.

Tachileik addicts inject by candlelight.

Author in Mong Hsat.

Footage captured inside the jungle. A rebel takes arms against an oppressive regime.

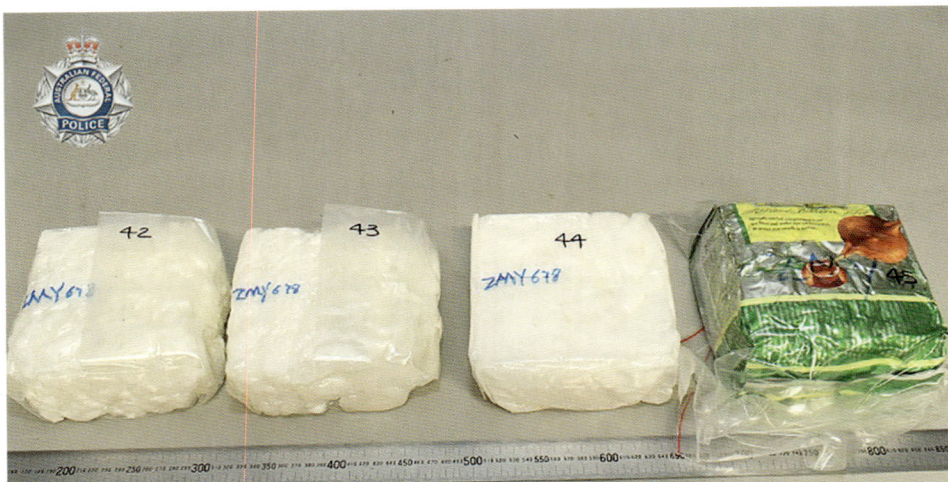

Four kilograms of green tea–packet crystalised methamphetamine from Wa State seized by the Australian Federal Police. *AFP*

Kings Cross Medically Supervised Injecting Centre, Sydney. *Uniting NSW*

can run through the days and nights for a week or two to produce that much meth. Each kilogram is carefully weighed and packaged for export in a green-tea package. The man says that he doesn't know how it reaches Australia, only that he sends it to a place outside Tachileik and from there it is smuggled over the border into Laos. It fits exactly with the story that I was told by the smugglers I met at the Lao border.

The remainder of the video focuses on a pile of finished product, maybe 100 kilograms of ice. In any case it's more ice than I've ever seen in one place. It seems bizarre to me that a kilometre or so from where we are now, in a corner of a cave in a dirt-poor corner of a war-torn jungle, there is a pile of drugs that would be worth more than $100 million in Sydney.

'Who owns all this?' I ask. 'Who is making the money from this ice?'

Michael shifts uneasily in his seat.

'I will not translate this question,' he says. 'He will not say.'

'And you, Michael? Will you say?'

'The one who owns this machine,' Michael says. His eyes narrow and he points his thin index finger at me. 'The one who owns this machine, he is Wa.'

This is the smoking gun that I've travelled halfway around the world to find. The UWSA and their political wing, the United Wa State Party (UWSP), have consistently denied that they have any involvement in meth production. Of course, agencies such as the UNODC and the AFP have called this out as untrue but still the Wa have maintained their line in the absence of hard evidence. Well, here is that evidence.

Michael and I don't talk much on the way back out of the jungle. The adrenaline that's been coursing through us is now spent. We both know the risks that we've taken to come here. For a minute, I wonder if I will ever see Michael again after I leave Myanmar. His courage, his determination to see this job through, are admirable. Maybe our attitude to danger is quite similar, and I can certainly empathise with Michael's bloody-minded determination to see something through to the end. It's what drives me too.

Over the past months that Michael and I have worked together on this story, we've encountered obstacles, not least the secret police who have blocked us, followed us, questioned us. More than once, Michael has displayed a defiance towards them, calling them out, defending his right to work with 'his client'. I am his client. I am paying Michael for his time, but I think this story represents more than that to him. He is personally invested in this, prepared to risk his life, because he's had enough of being told where he can go and who he can talk with in his own country.

Maybe Michael represents a spirit in the Burmese people that could one day be harnessed to overthrow the dictators. Or perhaps his defiance is simply a manifestation of the frustration of a divided people who never resolve their differences and will forever be in a state of war with each other. Time will tell. In the meantime, I'm happy that this journey is over and that Michael and I are able to return to our families, to our lives—Michael to drive his taxi, me to write my story.

Meanwhile, what we've seen happening in the jungle will continue. The Wa will no doubt claim that what I have seen here is merely the actions of a rogue actor, a bad apple operating independently, beyond their control, but I don't believe that. During a war, in the middle of a conflict zone, where I can personally attest that every single movement you make is monitored, there are checkpoints at every major intersection, and papers and passports are reviewed by soldiers multiple times on every journey, it is simply not credible to claim ignorance of a meth lab in your own backyard.

It's a confusing feeling for me personally. I don't know whether to feel elated that I've found what I've spent so long looking for, or sad to be confronted with the cold reality that organised criminals have seemingly found the perfect crime. I can't see any way, short of military action, that will put this enterprise out of business. As long as there is demand for meth, something we'll look more closely at in the second part of this book, this jungle meth lab will operate day and night to meet it.

My own journey has reached a significant milestone. I've come to one end of the Meth Road, ground zero, the source of the drugs that will soon be for sale on the streets of Brisbane, Sydney and Melbourne. It seems incongruous, but here, deep in a Burmese jungle, is the place where drug lords exploit political turmoil to turn huge profits. This is where ordinary Burmese people work through the night in a makeshift factory for a hundred dollars a week as though they were making television sets or stitching t-shirts.

Meth production in Myanmar is a world apart from Chris's shake-and-bake operation in Queensland, even

153

from the larger box labs designed by Dale Francis Drake. This is where supply is conducted on an industrial scale, using industrial equipment to process industrially produced precursor chemicals. A lab of this size can produce hundreds of kilograms in a single week. There are more than 150,000 square kilometres of jungle in Shan State just like this, where meth labs can be concealed in territory controlled by the UWSA or another rebel militia.

As mentioned earlier, there is nothing inherently stronger about P2P-produced meth compared to meth distilled from ephedrine or pseudoephedrine, but this production route brings the purity close to 100 per cent, which in effect means the same thing. This should worry us because higher-grade methamphetamine on the streets will inevitably take a toll.

This is where I want to turn my attention next. The last few months have given me a much better understanding of how the supply of methamphetamine operates—the production, the transport, the distribution. Now it's time to flip our attention to the demand side of the drug business.

I want to return to Australia and follow the Meth Road again, only this time in the opposite direction. I want to see how the demand for meth generates the need for jungle labs in the first place. Who are the people using and how is Australian society affected by the drugs that are being made here in Myanmar? These are important questions and the answers to them will inform how we move forward, how we shape our thinking about meth in the future.

It was my intention to leave Myanmar, cross the border back into Thailand and board a flight directly for Australia. But when I returned from the jungle, news reports told me that international flights were getting cancelled, and countries were closing their borders and recommending that nationals return to their own countries while they could. A mysterious illness that began in China was starting to spread beyond its borders and people were genuinely worried about it.

PART TWO

DEMAND

7

DARK FORCES

In January 2020, stories began to appear in the news of a mystery virus affecting people in China. The first time I realised that it was spreading beyond China's borders was when a concierge in Yangon used a digital scanner to take my temperature as I walked into the hotel lobby. Friends back home emailed to ask if I was okay. Another friend in Bangkok called to say that he was flying back to London while he still could. At first, that seemed alarmist; we all know now it wasn't. I decided I had no choice but to do the same and so, reluctantly, I took a flight back to London.

Over the next eighteen months, things began to change all over the world. Nationwide lockdowns threatened to destroy trade networks between countries. Governments struggled to keep ports open and even supermarket shelves started to empty of products that hitherto would have been refilled daily. I wondered how the meth industry in Myanmar was coping when multinational supply chains were struggling. Would the world re-emerge to the old status quo or would everything be changed forever?

Then things in Myanmar took an even greater turn for the worse. As if a global pandemic wasn't enough for the people to cope with, the Myanmar Army launched another coup in February 2021, declaring the election they had lost in November 2020 as unsound, ousting Aung San Suu Kyi from power and re-establishing themselves as the only party of government in Myanmar

From locked-down London, I read how, one by one, ethnic armed groups from the Karen to the Kachin and Shan rose up in defiance. During 2021, hostilities resumed to a level not seen for a decade. Hundreds of innocent people died and thousands were displaced—running from the violence, their homes bombed from the air, their villages burned to the ground.

Foolishly, I thought that the resumption of hostilities might be bad for the meth business. How could anyone continue to produce meth where there was a war going on? After the government officially closed the borders, it looked like the smuggling end of the business would be dead and buried. But I was wrong. Very wrong.

Covid and a Burmese coup were not the only major events to happen in early 2021. Another was the arrest of Tse Chi Lop, the head of the Sam Gor crime network, believed to be behind as much as half of Myanmar's meth exports. You might have expected his arrest to have slowed down the organisation's activities but, just as Al Qaeda didn't stop when Osama bin Laden was killed, Sam Gor seems to have recovered from Tse Chi Lop's demise and is already back exporting ice to Australia by the tonne.

Covid, the coup and Tse Chi Lop's arrest were no more than hiccups for those producing meth in Myanmar. Text messages back and forth with Michael confirmed that although prices in Tachileik fell dramatically from US$10,000 per kilo to $5000 or less, the big labs were still knocking out product. At first I couldn't understand how they were sourcing the chemicals that they needed to cook. The Chinese border was closed from the Chinese side and, officially, they weren't allowing shipments through.

But it seemed that the cooks had already started to prepare before the borders closed. While I was looking for flights back to London, the cooks were amassing stockpiles of precursor chemicals in case of problems with their supply lines. They were able to use those stockpiles during the Covid hiatus and now the borders are opening again, the supply lines have reopened. Even better, the coup created the perfect distraction for their ongoing illicit activities in Shan.

'If I was a meth producer, I'd be feeling pretty happy with the coup,' Richard Horsey, a Myanmar expert and former UN adviser, tells me. 'On all fronts, it's made life slightly easier.'

Richard says that parts of northern Shan State are a little bit edgier now, fighting is sporadic and air raids not uncommon, but southern and eastern Shan, including the areas controlled by the Wa, are relatively quiet. Various ethnic armed groups are using the conflict to reposition themselves strategically while they wait to see how things pan out in Yangon.

'They've all been kind of trying to take advantage of things to put their forces more on the front foot,' says Richard. 'But in Shan, things are relatively free from all-out fighting because when there's no fighting, everyone goes, "Great, let's make some money."'

Meanwhile the UWSA has expanded its territory. By staying out of the current conflict, it has seized an opportunity to build a new road between its territories in the north and south, effectively unifying the lands in between. Richard believes that very soon, the Wa will control one single patch of Shan from the Chinese border in the east to the Thai border in the south. In one move, the Wa will have linked their unfettered access to precursor chemicals in China with their well-trodden routes to international markets via Thailand and Laos. I would expect to see their control of the methamphetamine export market expand accordingly.

———

As the world started to open up again, and I realised that meth production inside Myanmar was as strong as ever, I turned my eyes back to Australia. Reports of seizures at international ports seemed to be as common as ever, suggesting that this peculiar phenomenon of a war-torn South-East Asian country fuelling the ongoing drug consumption of a developed nation thousands of kilometres away was as relevant as it had ever been. I wondered if the pandemic had changed things there at all.

Something that Australia does brilliantly, and which more countries could learn from, is analyse its wastewater for signs of drug use. The wastewater from the population's urine and faeces contains traces of metabolites from drugs which are detected at fifty sites across the country, including every major city, covering 57 per cent of the population—more than 14 million Australians. The multimillion-dollar project is by far the most extensive in the world and produces data that is the envy of researchers in other countries.

Australia's wastewater samples are routinely analysed to determine the concentrations of drug residues, including methamphetamine, from which estimates of population-wide drug use can be extrapolated. Even excluding the vast areas of the country where people rely on their own septic tanks, the analysis shows how national consumption of meth was rising dramatically year on year before the Covid-19 pandemic began. In 2018–19, the third year of the program, approximately 11.5 tonnes of methamphetamine was detected in the waste, up from 8.5 tonnes two years before, and equivalent to around 4 per cent of the adult population consuming meth at least once a month.

The wastewater analysis shows how methamphetamine has the highest consumption levels of any of the illicit stimulants available in Australia—more than double that of cocaine and ten times that of heroin. Both in capital cities and regional sites, meth use was growing faster than use of any other drugs too. It points to the fact that meth use was on the rise at a rate of about 17 per cent annually, despite record seizures at the border by the Australian Border Force and the AFP.

I was interested to see what the wastewater analysis showed about methamphetamine consumption during the pandemic. Would the inevitable interruption of trade flows that resulted from the closure of state borders, lockdowns and curfews have any effect on the consumption levels of the drug?

What the wastewater analysis showed provides a fascinating insight into that question. The data for August 2019 to August 2020 is interesting, as roughly half of the data falls in the pre-Covid era and half is in the Covid era. Over that period, the amount of methamphetamine appearing in the wastewater suggests that consumption remained roughly consistent with pre-Covid levels at just over 11 tonnes.

The following year's data, covering August 2020 to August 2021, however, shows that something very different was going on. Methamphetamine consumption dropped to under 9 tonnes—a reduction in national consumption of more than 20 per cent.

So why did it take so long after the pandemic began for the consumption levels to drop? I put that question to Cameron Francis, CEO of The Loop Australia, a nonprofit organisations that supports drug-checking services in Australia. The Loop were constantly checking and monitoring the drugs on the street during the whole period.

Cameron says that he believes the anomaly can best be explained by stockpiling. 'Brisbane had an immediate drop in meth as soon as lockdown number one happened,' he says. 'Whereas in regional Queensland, the meth levels stayed really high until the next six-month period.'

The reason for that, Cameron believes, is that regional areas were being used for meth storage before the pandemic began. Over the lockdown period, those stores were gradually run down by dealers servicing the local communities. 'By the time the next lockdown's come along,' Cameron says, 'it's all been used up, everyone's taken it and now it's gone.'

This raises an interesting issue for me. If the interruption in supply routes created by Covid-19 could create a 20 per cent drop in consumption nationally, then isn't that evidence that high-level supply constraints can have an effect on usage? The bigger question is whether those effects are lasting. Fortunately, the good people who run the National Wastewater Drug Monitoring Program have produced another report since that answers that question.

The latest annual data I accessed at time of writing, which covers the first mostly post-Covid period of August 2021 to August 2022, found that meth consumption was on the rise again, back over 9 tonnes, but only just. Nothing like the 11.5 tonnes seen before the pandemic. Time will tell whether this is sustained but for now, while methamphetamine use is still huge, it certainly looks like it has been reduced by the indirect effects of Covid on the supply chain.

Still, any increase in national methamphetamine use at a time when the cost of living has never been higher is concerning. Despite the fact that Australians are increasingly constrained in their disposable income, they still found an estimated $8 billion to spend on methamphetamine between August 2021 and August 2022. Methamphetamine now accounts for 83 per cent of all the money spent on illegal drugs (excluding cannabis) by Australians. The issue has certainly not gone away.

The annual Illicit Drug Data Reports published by the Australian Criminal Intelligence Commission show

how seizures were affected by the pandemic. In the year 2017–18, nearly 3 tonnes of 'amphetamine-type stimulants', the majority of them methamphetamine, were seized at Australia's borders. The following year, 2018–19, that figure rose a whopping 74 per cent to more than 5 tonnes. By any measure, this was a phenomenal performance by the AFP and the Australian Border Force. That means they were intercepting around one-third of all the meth coming into the country.

Interestingly, these interceptions seem to be priced into the market. The price of meth during this time stayed pretty level, which means that seizures were neither higher nor lower than the market expected. It's likely that without those seizures, 30 per cent more meth would have hit the streets, prices would have dropped and consumption would have increased.

During the pandemic, consumption fell and prices rose. What happened to seizures at the border during that time? In 2019–20, the year that spanned the start of Covid border closures, big seizures dominated the headlines. In Melbourne, when counter-narcotics police intercepted a shipment of over 1.5 tonnes concealed in stereo speakers sent from Thailand, overall interceptions were still over 5 tonnes, slightly up from the previous year. Without those kind of interceptions, dealers wouldn't have needed to use up their stockpiles during the pandemic, so the effect was certainly felt by the gangs. Covid did a lot of damage to their supply chains from which it might take years to recover.

And yet, as the borders reopened, these huge interceptions of methamphetamine seemed to have been just enough to maintain the status quo, enough to stop the situation getting worse, but not enough to make it better. The pandemic had an effect but use is on the rise again. It is business as usual out there on the Meth Road.

As I realised that meth production inside Myanmar was still strong, and usage back on the rise again in Australia, I knew that the problem was as real as ever. I packed a bag and booked myself a flight to the other side of the world. It was time to return to Australia and investigate how Asian methamphetamine was influencing Australian society—and, crucially, what could be done about it.

8

ALL PR IS BAD PR

A young man in his early thirties is escorted into the emergency room at the local hospital by two police officers. As they pass through the door, the man is approached by a concerned-looking medic who begins to ask him if he's okay. But before the doctor can finish the question, the man headbutts him in the face, knocking him to the floor. Immediately, he tosses the two police officers aside with super-heroic strength before he picks up a chair and hurls it at a window. 'Ice destroys lives,' says the narrator. 'Don't let it destroy yours.'

This public health advert was one of many that were produced for the Australian government and distributed on national television in prime time. The aim was to change the narrative on meth by employing the kind of scare tactics used on cigarette packets that proved to be so successful at reducing smoking rates.

When I first saw the advert, I was left asking, 'What happened next?' I understood that the purpose of the campaign was to scare off would-be meth users from trying the drug, to paint a picture so bleak that even the idea of meth was abhorrent. But what about the poor man in the advert? What happened to him? He's distressed, in a terrifying state of psychosis, and in need of help. He's arrived at what should be a safe place, a hospital no less, and yet nothing in the advert seeks to reassure us that he's going to be okay.

I'm rewatching the advert on my laptop in an Airbnb in Brisbane, having flown halfway across the world to resume my journey along the Meth Road. I've chosen to pick up the trail in Queensland for a number of reasons. First, I feel that Queensland is the spiritual home of Australian meth, the place where Dale Francis Drake first invented a way for amateur chemists to produce quality product with the formula he developed in his shed in Gympie. Second, I want to see more than simply what is happening in Sydney and Melbourne.

I'm going to make a journey through the country, starting in Brisbane, then heading south, stopping at towns and cities along the way, trying to get a flavour for how methamphetamine is affecting people through the country—the Australian leg of the Meth Road, if you like.

But first, the TV advert is still troubling me and so I've arranged to speak to someone who can talk firsthand about what it is like to arrive in an ER while high on ice. A mutual friend has put me in touch with Shawnee, who's agreed to meet me for coffee.

170

'I voluntarily took myself to the hospital because I was in psychosis,' says Shawnee when we meet at the local coffee shop. Shawnee is remembering a nightmare evening they experienced three years ago after smoking ice. 'I was terrified. Absolutely terrified.'

Thankfully, Shawnee's fine now. As we sit and sip lattes, they can chat happily about their drug history. Shawnee is thirty-one, bright, educated and very articulate. They have agreed to relay their experience of using meth, warts and all, and they openly admit that it isn't all positive, as turning up at the hospital in a state of acute psychosis attests. But Shawnee is determined to make the case that all people who use ice aren't bad.

The night Shawnee turned up at the ER, they were accompanied by their girlfriend. Shawnee wasn't behaving aggressively, not yelling or screaming, nor presenting a danger to themselves or anyone else, but still, instead of admitting them, the staff on the ward locked Shawnee in a storage cupboard where they remained for twelve hours.

'I ended up knocking my head—that's when this paralysis started to take hold. I couldn't move. My face was crying, tears were coming out, but I couldn't speak, couldn't do anything like that,' Shawnee says.

It sounds like abuse, the kind of experience that would leave anyone scarred. Shawnee believes that the reason they were treated this way comes down to adverts like the one I'd seen, campaigns that seem to paint all people who use drugs with the same brush.

'If we use drugs, we must be addicts—and once an addict, always an addict,' Shawnee says.

The stigmatisation logic follows from there—addicts are all uneducated, from low socioeconomic brackets and broken homes. It follows then that they are viewed as dirty and undignified, not worthy of the same care and respect as people whose vices are caffeine, nicotine or alcohol.

Every year the NSW government sends out an anonymous survey to its hospital staff, which aims to track stigma and discrimination among medical staff. The questionnaire asks nurses and doctors in the hospital systems about how they treat people who come in presenting with different conditions. So it might ask whether staff treat someone with, say, diabetes differently from someone with a sexually transmitted infection, or a history of IV drug use, or in psychosis.

The results surprised me because they show how nurses and doctors, people who I had thought would understand the complexities of drug use better than most, admitted that they were treating patients differently if they came in as drug users.

Meth and heroin users tend to be vilified the most, which is less surprising I suppose if you consider the TV advert. Shawnee says their meth use began fifteen years ago when they were sixteen. By twenty-one Shawnee had had their first experience of rehab, the first of five goes before they got a handle on it.

'It took me a long time of backing and forthing to move away from dependency to where I could use recreationally. Now I have a healthy appreciation for drugs, as opposed to using drugs to escape, to fix everything.'

For years, Shawnee says they used daily while working days as a disability support worker and studying veterinary nursing in the evenings. Nobody noticed. They were able to drift through life, surrounded by co-workers who remained oblivious to the fact that Shawnee was consuming a couple of points before work in much the same way as anyone else might have a couple of cups of tea.

'To be honest, I wouldn't be surprised if I'm an undiagnosed ADHD'—attention deficit hyperactivity disorder—'and that I used meth as a way to help me function. But I started using after I was sexually assaulted aged fifteen.'

This sentence contains the double whammy as far as my experience of interviewing meth users is concerned. I'm yet to meet someone who hasn't explained their meth use in one of these two contexts.

Time and again while researching this book, I've met adults with no diagnosed history of childhood ADHD but who now either suspect or have been told that they have ADHD. The source of their information seems to be a combination of popular media influencers and private ADHD specialists who charge people looking for a diagnosis around $600 an hour to give them one.

I do think it's fair to say that more and more people are struggling to cope within our society but it seems strange to me that so many could have gone so long undiagnosed in one of the most medicated societies in the world. Is it plausible that all of a sudden such a huge number of adults are developing a childhood condition in adulthood?

It's not only in Australia that people are asking this question. A recent undercover investigation in London by the BBC's *Panorama* found that a number of private clinics handed out ADHD diagnoses after brief online consultations to its journalist who didn't have the condition. How many more people could have been wrongly told that they have ADHD and prescribed medication for it?

Whatever the answer, it seems perverse to me that we are simultaneously increasing the legitimisation of some stimulants while stigmatising other stimulants that operate in very similar ways.

'How you take legal stimulants might be different to meth, but they are the same drug,' Sam, a psychiatric doctor, tells me. 'You get prescribed thirty or forty-five milligrams of dexamphetamine and that's like using a point of meth every day.'

If any of us came across someone who said they were taking a point of meth every day, we'd say they had a problem. Right? We'd assume they had a serious drug-dependency issue. But because dexamphetamine is prescribed, we look at it entirely differently. Anyone who can afford the private consultation fee is sheltered from the stigma that a meth user, who is maybe self-medicating for the same set of symptoms, the same feelings, has to negotiate.

So I'm not surprised to hear Shawnee use this language. It's understandable that they would believe there is a self-medication element to their meth use. That's entirely consistent with what they see all around them. And isn't it easier to feel like you're part of something bigger rather than an outlier, someone different from the norm?

Although Shawnee's meth use grew to be far from normal. They ended up staying awake for nine days at a time, then crashing out, then being up for another eight or nine days, then crashing out again. The psychosis that level of use was causing was becoming more and more intense.

'The time between my psychoses was getting shorter and the length of them getting longer,' Shawnee says. 'I was hearing things, seeing dark figures in my peripheral vision—men wearing hats, and trenchcoats with the lapels pulled up.'

Whenever they'd see the dark figures, Shawnee would go to bed and eat something. This was the only way to prevent slipping deeper into the psychosis and experiencing more hallucinations. They knew then that their drug use had moved from recreational to something more dependent but they also felt incredibly isolated.

'I was like, "Oh shit, people view me differently now because this is a drug I use every day. People have made up their minds about me without even speaking to me."'

And that included the medical professionals at the local hospital. It is a problem when people whose meth use has become problematic don't feel as though there's anywhere safe to turn. However one feels about meth as a drug, civilised society has to find a way to deal with those who have found themselves in danger and distress—especially if they are asking for help.

———

Someone who knows what she's using ice for is Karly, a mid-thirties university graduate and mother of two who is in Brisbane for a work conference and enjoying a couple of nights away from the kids. We meet in a bar in the evening and she says that she intends to let her hair down while she can. When I ask her if that could include taking some ice, she answers with a smile, 'Probably.'

Karly moved to Queensland after her master's program to work in drug and alcohol services focused on harm reduction. She says that services like hers desperately need people who are educated and who have some privilege to speak up for people who can't.

Karly is both of those things—privileged and educated— but she says that since moving from Western Australia to Queensland, she has, at times, found working in her field to be a disheartening experience.

'Queensland is so behind the times,' she sighs. 'The government is so conservative, very Christian based. They basically want to stick all the junkies and gays in a rocket and shoot them off into space.'

As a non-Australian, I've been surprised by just how independent the individual states are of each other and how little the federal government can effect policy in areas like drugs. The proliferation of ice, produced in or smuggled into one part of the country and distributed nationally, seems to me to present a good argument for having a nationwide strategy to deal with it.

Australia's drug policy has long been based on a broad mix of policies to reduce supply, reduce demand and minimise harm, but each state has control over where their priorities lie. Legislation is state based so different states can apply different penalties to different drugs.

For example, South Australia, the ACT and the Northern Territory have decriminalised cannabis use, replacing criminal convictions for users with civil penalties and fines. But in any of the other states, you can still get a criminal record for being caught with even a personal quantity of marijuana.

Karly agrees that these discrepancies seem arbitrary and unfair, although the national strategy that she'd like to see is a controversial one.

'I want to see meth legalised,' she says. 'A drug is a drug. That's it. White Australian males drink alcohol. It's a very Aussie bloke thing.'

Karly is an open poly-drug user, which means that as well as recreationally taking methamphetamine she also enjoys using ecstasy, cannabis and magic mushrooms. When she was eighteen she got into heroin but then moved back to Perth where there was a lot of meth. That was when she switched from shooting heroin to shooting meth.

Karly cites Australia's harm-minimisation strategy around heroin as an example of where a national policy can make a positive difference. In the 1980s, when the daughter of Australian prime minister Bob Hawke got hooked on heroin, the government engaged with the issue nationally. Because heroin was a personal issue for Hawke—he didn't want to see his daughter die—he made it a priority to change the policy for all Australians.

The policies that Bob Hawke championed brought all the state governments together for a moment in time. Together they introduced policies for needle exchanges that profoundly reduced the spread of HIV, established regular national surveys, and formed a ministerial council on drug strategy that led to the country producing some of the most comprehensive drug data in the world. In the 1990s, Australia led the world in its progressive drug policies.

But since then, the tough-on-drugs narrative has crept back. Successive governments in Australia have lurched further and further from harm-reduction strategies and more towards law enforcement strategies.

Yet there are now more Australian daughters and sons than ever before who have problems with drugs. It seems incredible that it took a personal tragedy in the prime minister's family to get the government to rethink its drug policy in the first place. It seems to be parochial and nepotistic policymaking in anyone's book. But it's even more surprising that policies which resulted in fewer people dying didn't last. Campaigners like Karly find it frustrating when the data suggests that there had been so much success from harm minimisation as a drug strategy back then.

'Drug use is criminalised and all the government's money goes to supply reduction—police, justice, customs. Just a waste of so much money while people get hurt.'

Australia's strategy to deal with drugs isn't actually solely based on policing. It is certainly focused on supply reduction (targeting criminal gangs who produce and distribute), but there is also money assigned to demand reduction (adverts and campaigns that put people off taking drugs), drug treatment (rehab and counselling) and harm reduction (helping drug users to minimise the dangers of using drugs). However currently, the supply-reduction side of the strategy absorbs the vast majority of budgets at both the national and state level.

The national drugs and alcohol budget assigns over 65 per cent to law enforcement and less than 5 per cent to harm reduction. More progressive countries such as

Portugal have worked hard to switch this around, reallocating money from law enforcement into health and harm-reduction strategies. As a result, fewer people are dying. Yet there is still a lot of resistance to enforcing a similar policy change in Australia.

'It's still "tough on drugs, tougher on drug users", all that bollocks,' says Karly. 'I've lost so many friends that didn't need to die, so many times that I could have died from dirty shots.'

Karly claims that backyard cooks, like Chris who we met in chapter one, don't know what they're doing and that the chemicals they're accessing to produce meth in their kitchens aren't healthy. Having seen it with my own eyes, it's hard to disagree. There's no way in the world, even if I were a meth user, that I'd inject the meth from Chris's shake-and-bake lab. But Karly says that there's often no choice. She says that users are forced into such risky behaviours by having to keep their use a secret. That shame risks killing people.

'They're splitting shit with diesel and using lubricant now to cut it because it's nice and heavy.' Karly winces as she describes it to me. 'Sure, the gear feels nice and heavy but then you put it in a pipe and you can see the sludge. But people are having to put this shit in their bodies because they keep outlawing the basic ingredients that you need to cook this stuff.'

Karly argues that impurities cause deaths, which could be avoided if the production of meth was regulated. In her vision of the future, Australian authorities sanction and regulate the production of lovely, clean, pure methamphetamine that is available on the open market to users.

'We use drugs. That's just what we do,' she says. 'I have a seven-year-old and a five-year-old and I just don't want to see them in harm's way, where they have to experiment with dangerous chemicals for no good reason than some fucking chump who enjoys alcohol and coke, which is now legal in the ACT, who deems meth to be a worse drug.'

Karly's referring to the fact that possession of a personal quantity of cocaine has been decriminalised in the ACT, where most of Australia's federal lawmakers work. But such 'enlightenment' hasn't spread out across the rest of Australia, where getting caught with a bag of ice will land you with a conviction that will remain on your record for life.

Karly's determined to change all that. 'I understand this is going to take years and years and years, but a drug's a drug,' she says. 'If we can just have clean drugs so no one needs to die, isn't that a no-brainer?'

I don't think so. I can see her logic in terms of direct harm minimisation—meth produced in a government-sanctioned lab would undoubtedly be cleaner than Chris's combination of ice packs and camping gas but I can't help but feel that Karly is also missing something fundamental.

———

To get to the bottom of what that is, I drive out to a quiet café on the outskirts of East Gosford, north of Sydney, where I meet Mark. I've read a little about Mark in the press but I'm excited to hear his story firsthand. Karly and Shawnee aside, many—indeed most—of the meth users that I've encountered in Asia and Australia so far have been what you might generously describe as 'down on their luck'. The users at the soup kitchen in Southport, just like the addicts in Tachileik, seemed to be lost in a spiral of addiction and destitution. I had a sense from all of them that there was a kind of tragic inevitability to their stories that often stemmed from having lived through quite challenging circumstances.

But I'm meeting with Mark today because I think his story offers another view of who is consuming meth in Australia—middle-class users, those who society would deem 'successful' people, who have enjoyed partaking in meth recreationally. I want to hear their stories too because I feel that if their experiences are what they seem to be, they might put paid to the perception that meth is something 'bogan', reserved for Australia's underclass, the elixir of the homeless and destitute.

When I hear the sound of my name, I look up from my coffee and realise that Mark is exactly what I've been looking for. He looks like the kind of guy who I might see at my local golf club—sixty-ish, stocky, dressed in a smart pair of chinos, with an expensive shirt tucked into his belt. He drops the keys to his BMW on the table before he shakes my hand with the confidence of a man who knows how to create a strong first impression. Mark doesn't need to say anything for me to know that he's wealthy. He oozes confidence, charm and privilege.

He orders himself a latte and wastes no time in getting into his story. There's no small talk. Mark has come to meet me with a purpose and I feel like his time is valuable, and he's going to make every second count. Before I even ask him to, he launches into telling me about his past.

'I had a big job,' he says, sipping his latte. 'I was CEO of a big food distribution network with sixty-four outlets around Australia and hundreds of employees. When I started the job, the group was turning over four hundred million dollars; when I finished, it was turning over eight hundred million. It was a very successful business.'

It seems impossible that this guy is a meth user. The gulf between the man sitting opposite me and the delusional users, lost in the fog of psychosis, who I met in Southport is wider than an ocean. Mark looks exactly like the man he just described. Nothing in me questions the veracity of what he's just told me because he looks like a CEO, he talks like a CEO, and—I did my research—he was indeed a CEO. And yet . . .

'What I hadn't realised about myself was that I'd got burned out and I should've stopped work a couple of years before I did,' he says.

Mark explains how four years ago, a couple of years into the new job, he and his wife bought a property. There were problems associated with the building and, on top of his work, he was having fights with a big insurance company. There was just a lot going on in his life.

'It turned out I was more vulnerable than I realised,' he says.

Then things went up another level. Mark engaged a small boutique firm of consultants to come in and overhaul the company's IT systems. They were highly qualified, high-achieving, dynamic young professionals with a reputation for working hard and playing harder. For a guy like Mark who already worked ninety hours a week minimum, he was drawn to their ethic.

'I picked them because they were the best,' he says.

Part of winning the tender included a commitment to turn around the job on a very tight timetable. The deal that Mark had negotiated with them was that if they ran over then they would lose half the money—more than half a million dollars.

'They started to run late,' Mark says, 'and so they asked me if I would conduct review meetings at night. I started to go to their offices after work, often working into the small hours. One night, one of them pulled out this little pipe. It sounds very naive now, but I didn't even know what it was.'

Of course, it was a meth pipe. Up until that point, Mark had thought meth was something only used by truck drivers and sex workers. He never imagined for a moment that the kind of high-achieving, smart people he was working with would use meth. For a man whose only vice was the occasional glass of wine, the idea of taking drugs was entirely alien. He politely declined when the pipe was offered to him.

But then one night, Mark says that he was feeling particularly flat, tired, struggling to stay awake and keep up with the others. The pressure of his work deadline was increasing—Mark had put himself on the line with his board when he chose to overhaul the IT and bring in the consultants. He felt invested in the project's success and saw how the consultants could work long hours and still produce quality work. When he was offered the pipe again, he decided to give it a try. He took his first puff.

'The effect was instant,' he remembers. 'I was like the man with the Energizer batteries in me.'

Mark said that he liked that feeling. He found it helpful, giving him the energy he'd been lacking. He did it again. Initially, he only smoked meth when he was working at the consultants' offices. For Mark, meth was a work enhancer, a magic potion that he could take when needed to help him deliver the project on time. He says not only could he work longer, but his output was of a higher quality.

I've heard similar claims being made by meth users. They usually cite stories about Japanese kamikaze pilots or about Adolf Hitler, who was said to get a shot of meth from his physician every day. I'm not sure either of those examples proves that productivity was enhanced by the drug. In fact, the current research on meth's effects on productivity in healthy people doesn't support the idea either. A recent paper presented by the University of Melbourne found that not only does meth not increase overall cognitive performance in healthy individuals, but it may even reduce productivity. Yet that doesn't stop people who are on meth from perceiving that the opposite is true. Like the kamikaze pilots, Mark felt that his productivity was enhanced and that was all that mattered.

'I thought I'd be alright,' Mark says. 'I believed I was a man who didn't have an addictive personality. Some people would say I was a workaholic, maybe, but I would say I just did what needed to be done to be successful.'

Mark wasn't born with a silver spoon in his mouth. His grandfather was a foreman of a zinc works. His parents both came from the same sort of working-class families and though he says they were both smart, they weren't formally well educated. Mark went into business straight from school and after landing a job in the NSW public service, he went to university to do a degree in accounting and computing science.

Twenty years in the NSW public service, working his way through the ranks, set him up for a move to the private sector in senior management. He worked across various industries, thriving in every post before eventually settling into his role as CEO at his last company. Mark describes himself as 'self-made', a community-minded Rotarian and an upstanding pillar of his community—albeit one who had started to develop a meth habit.

When his work project ended (delivered on time), there was a party to celebrate, and Mark agreed to pop in for a quick drink to congratulate the team on a job well done. But by that point, he'd already started smoking a little meth outside of work. He didn't realise yet that he was becoming hooked on the drug. Then came the moment when everything turned.

'I let someone inject me,' he says ruefully. 'If you'd have said to me six months before that, "How about I inject you with something?", I would have just said, "Do you want me to poke your eyes out?"'

So that was the moment Mark knew his meth use had become something else. Within eight weeks of first smoking the drug, he let a woman he barely know inject him with it. She showed him the whole ritual—getting the meth ready, locating a vein—and after that, he didn't need help anymore. He was intoxicated to a completely new level. He could now inject himself, and he began to spiral downward.

Mark says that his wife was kept completely in the dark. With the family home being located on the NSW Central Coast and the company office in Parramatta, in Sydney's west, Mark had rented an apartment so that he could crash when working late. 'I just came up with all sorts of comfortable stories, why it was not a good idea for my wife to come down during the week.'

One of the stories he had to explain was how he had lost so much weight. Mark, who used to weigh 95 kilos, was now down to 72 kilos. A couple of friends thought he had cancer. He told everyone that he'd gone nuts on a new diet and was running every morning.

When he came home late on Friday nights, he told his wife that he was exhausted from work and would often sleep most of the weekend. Like any spouse in the same position, Mark's wife never once imagined that her CEO husband was, in fact, sleeping off a meth hangover. For seven months, Mark used meth from Monday to Friday and then crashed at weekends in Gosford without arousing any suspicion.

But down in Sydney, things were slowly getting out of hand. Mark, a hugely successful businessman, brought many of those skills to his new life of drugs. Not content with paying premium prices for small quantities on the street, he sought out the big-time dealers who offered discounts for buying in bulk. He took the same approach to meth that he took to multimillion-dollar commercial deals. After getting ripped off by one of his dealers, Mark decided to go straight to the source.

'I found my way to one of the big drug-gang families. A Lebanese family,' he says. 'Some of the people I dealt with have since been murdered in gangland wars in the area down there. I just went [to them] and said, "Listen, I'm a businessman and you run a shit show. I'll set up a much better distribution system and I'll sell it at a price that you won't be able to match. Unless you sort this shit out and make sure that never happens to me again." And they did.'

Mark started taking bigger and bigger quantities from the Lebanese family, getting into the party scene, passing on meth to other people he was hanging around with. He says a lot of things happened that he's not proud of, things that even now he'd rather not talk about. He was becoming increasingly paranoid, convinced that he was being tracked by the cops. He even enlisted a private security firm to do a bug sweep of his apartment.

While Mark could mask his addiction from his wife, his kids weren't quite so easy to fool. His son, a police officer in Queensland, suspected that something was amiss and sent a couple of colleagues to go and check on his dad. They visited Mark before they called his son with the bad news.

'They told him, "Your dad's shooting up ice and he's off his head,"' Mark says, looking a little ashamed.

The description was a fair one. The psychosis Mark was experiencing was frequent and sometimes extreme. He was hallucinating and seeing things that weren't there. He would go stomping through the bush barefoot, climb mountains and walk huge distances without knowing how he'd got to a destination.

'One time, I was driving up the Newcastle freeway at 110 kilometres per hour when suddenly the road was full of people facing me,' he remembers. 'There were people behind people behind people behind people. Marching not in army uniforms but in all sorts of different clothes with very discrete faces. I lifted my foot off the accelerator and tried to slam on the brake. I thought, "Jesus, if I drive in, I'll kill them" but as I got closer and closer, they all just disappeared.'

Mark says that he never found his hallucinations frightening, rather he felt that they fed into a sense that he was searching for something. The more dissociated he became from his real life, the closer he thought he was getting to what he was looking for. And he realised that the better-quality product took him further, deeper into that unknown. He began to seek out the bigger, drier shards of ice that were coming in from Asia that took him higher.

An admirer of fine wine and cognac, Mark quickly became a connoisseur of meth. He had the means to buy the best product and he liked the good stuff that came from Asia, the kind being cooked in the jungles of Myanmar. He draws a graph with his fingers to describe the shape of the high, the profile of the experience.

'You'll get a little tiny rush. And then it just creeps on, creeps on, creeps on as the intensity of the effect slowly rises.' He looks a little wistful as he remembers it, as though he's recalling a particularly fine bottle of claret that he drank with a steak once.

Several months after Mark started injecting meth, his family staged an intervention. His kids and wife turned up at the door of his Sydney flat and put him under family arrest, confiscating his phone and whisking him away to Queensland. Mark's son discovered that Mark had upset the local bikie gang, who had heard he was dealing without their approval. While Mark contends he wasn't the dealer, the reality was that he was hiding his habit by buying ice once in bulk and then selling to people he was socialising with rather than risk regular withdrawals showing up on his bank statements.

Against Mark's will, his family insisted that he check into a residential rehab clinic. Mark describes it as the day of greatest shame in his whole life and yet he knows now that it came from a place of love. He was fortunate to have a family that loved him enough, and who had the resources to airlift him out of this situation and enter him voluntarily into a program.

During the month that Mark spent in rehab, doing daily therapy, he made an important discovery about his past, something that he'd buried since he was a child.

'I had to confront stuff from my past, stuff that I'd never talked about since I was a five-year-old,' he says. 'My parents ran a hotel with a gardener who had a shed down the back of the building. He groomed me and then molested me regularly for a year. I didn't realise the profound effect that had on me.'

I don't know why I'm surprised as Mark tells me the sad story of how he was systematically abused by a nefarious paedophile. Yet again, someone with dysfunctional methamphetamine use is describing to me a trauma in their past from which they were desperate to escape. Mark's illustrious career had offered him no protection from that pain. When the pain comes from within, it seems the dissociation offered by meth is hard to beat.

Not long after he left the health retreat, Mark started using again. It was intermittent at first, but then the cycles of time between stopping and starting got shorter and shorter until soon he was injecting daily again.

On a night when his supply ran dry, he arranged a pickup from a new dealer but, concerned that the dealer might try to rob him, he retrieved an unregistered gun from his safe. The deal never happened because a local police officer, passing on routine patrol, suspicious of Mark's vehicle parked at 3 a.m., came to investigate. Mark was charged with possession of a firearm and sentenced to a mandatory sixteen months: ten in jail and six on parole.

Prison was Mark's rock bottom and he stopped using inside, throwing himself into advocating for prisoners who lacked the literacy or education to do so for themselves, something he continues to do today.

Another thing he continues to do is meth. He shrugs when he tells me this.

'It's a very miserable experience,' he admits. 'I can drink wine, I can just about do anything I want to do, but nothing triggers that compulsion in me the way that crystal meth does.'

Hearing Mark say this—and, indeed, hearing all these firsthand stories from users—leaves me with a particular concern about meth and the potential for harm that it poses. The dangers of meth seem objectively greater than any other drugs that are in common circulation. Even alcohol on a per-user basis poses a lower risk than meth.

Having seen the experience of countries, like the US and Portugal, where cannabis has been decriminalised or even legalised, it's clear that societal meltdown was not the result. There is a compelling logic to try something similar in Australia beyond just the ACT. The millions and millions of dollars that are spent on policing the market for cannabis could be better spent on drugs that pose a greater danger. For me, that should always include meth.

I want to return to the issue of law enforcement in a later chapter, but for now, in terms of reducing the demand for ice, there is a need to provide reasonable education to drug users. Honesty is integral if you want to retain credibility. If all drugs are banned, and governments make out that everything is on equal footing in terms of the harm it causes, then governments risk coming across as ignorant to the very people who they're trying to educate.

But there's a line between singling out meth as a more destructive drug and singling out meth *users* as destructive individuals in a TV advertising campaign. There are more effective, less stigmatising and less hysterical ways to get the message across that meth use can quickly turn problematic in even the most educated and successful people in society.

Meth is not cannabis. It's not even MDMA or LSD. Shawnee, Mark and Karly are all educated, intelligent, productive members of society, and they demonstrate very well that meth has a potential for harm way beyond that of other drugs. But none of them has ever torn apart an ER room or attacked a doctor. Portraying meth users in this way risks obfuscating the real message that meth is an insidious and corrosive narcotic.

Meth does cause harm, and when it does, compassion and understanding need to be at the forefront. In the meantime, meth should not be part of any wider debate about legalising drugs.

But before we take a look at strategies for harm reduction and law enforcement specifically, I'd like to take a sideways step and look at how demand-reduction strategies are supported by one of Australia's growth industries: rehabilitation.

9

REHAB

'You're probably the first media request I've had in about four years,' says Luke Williams into the screen. I can see that he is lying on a metal-framed bed, and behind him is a wall devoid of pictures. Luke explains that he is into his fourth week of a residential rehabilitation program for addiction to methamphetamine.

A couple of years ago, I came across a fascinating book Luke had written about his descent into ice addiction. What started as an assignment for his employer, ABC Radio—an immersive exposé of how people with ice addiction lived in the suburbs of Melbourne—turned bad when Luke was drawn into using himself.

As a fellow journalist, I admired both the chutzpah of the book's premise and the fearless abandonment of personal safety in pursuit of the 'truth' of a story. I'd like to think that it's the kind of thing a younger me might have done. However, sadly for Luke, like a moth flying too close to the flame, he became hooked.

'I'm three weeks clean,' Luke says brightly and seems pretty upbeat, all things considered. 'I'm doing a twelve-week program and then I'll probably do a twelve-week program somewhere else.'

While researching his book in 2014, Luke moved in with an old high school friend whose boyfriend was an ice dealer. The easy proximity to supply and a culture of daily meth use was too much for him to resist and before long he was injecting. Somehow, he managed to finish the book despite the drugs.

'There's qualities about meth that lend itself to you being a good worker in a lot of ways,' he laughs. 'One is that it makes you very obsessive about things. So you can just be stuck in that one task and not do anything else. You don't need to eat, you don't need to sleep, you often don't need to go to the toilet.'

I imagine him leaning over his keyboard, typing frantically, a syringe by his side, knocking out copy to make his deadline. It makes total sense. Why would a writer be any different from, say, a Burmese long-distance lorry driver or a Thai tuk-tuk driver? Meth staves off tiredness and enables the user to work long hours. In careers where face-to-face social interaction is minimal, there's nobody around to notice that you're high.

It's no coincidence that meth use has risen alongside a rise in individualistic capitalism over the last twenty years. In lots of Asian countries, where hard work, long hours and putting aside everything else are key to success, meth use fits pretty well. In individualised cultures, a drug that celebrates individualism is a perfect fit. Meth is a drug that gets you through the night, the cold, the loneliness, and the hours and hours of grind needed to get the job done.

That's what Luke did. Once the book was written, he checked himself into rehab but quickly fell back into using again. Media outlets who wanted to do a story about ice would contact him and pretty soon he'd become 'the go-to meth guy', which he says now wasn't 'conducive to future career opportunities'. Feeling that he had no other option but to quit journalism, he signed up to do a law degree and landed a job at a good firm.

'I hated it,' he sighs. 'I just started using again because the world that meth created was so much more interesting and fulfilling than my everyday life. I started using every morning before I went to work and then finally I quit my job about a year and a half ago.'

He's been using it ever since. At least he was until three weeks before I spoke with him.

In 2020–21, around 33,000 people in Australia received treatment for methamphetamine use—slightly less than for alcohol. The majority of meth users treated were male (60 per cent) and the number skews towards the young—for people under forty, meth use was the most commonly treated drug use. Counselling is still the most popular treatment offered to users, while rehab numbers remain pretty level at approximately 14,000 treatments annually. However, that number is constrained by the number of places available.

The average amount of time spent in rehab by those 14,000 people was forty-three days, and the vast majority of these programs were residential. So the norm is that you go away to a place, like Luke did, for seven or eight weeks, where you receive counselling, withdrawal management and drug education. The ratio of people who complete treatment to those who leave early is approximately 3:1.

Anyone in Australia can set up a private rehab clinic. While some favour a military-style boot camp approach, others practise abstinence wrapped up with a religious or spiritual ideology. Some centres offer cognitive behavioural therapy to help 'reprogram' the brain, while others advocate a mindfulness-based approach to preventing relapse.

There are as many approaches as there are centres and the reporting on success rates can be unclear. One of the biggest issues the rehabilitation sector faces is the lack of regulation or transparency of treatment services. There is no way of knowing exactly how many private services are operating outside of the government-sponsored centres, and no systematic monitoring of what they do or their outcomes.

———

The Australian Anti Ice Campaign (AAIC) was established by former users who felt they could help others by sharing the wisdom they'd gleaned from coming off drugs themselves. The question of what constitutes a successful rehabilitation program remains a much debated one but the real test, at the end of the day, is how a former user manages their rehabilitation after they leave rehab. It's a lot harder to stay off meth when faced with all the old triggers that led you to it in the first place. The AAIC claims to be ahead of its rivals in this regard.

Andrea Simmons, ten years clean after two years as a full-time ice addict, runs the AAIC. When I meet her at the organisation's office, on an industrial estate just outside of the Gold Coast, she explains to me that they are specifically remitted to help secure and rehabilitate addicts of methamphetamine. I notice a very slight slur in her voice, which she says is a lasting side effect from her two years of using. Several MRI and CAT scans of her brain have revealed considerable damage to her amygdala, which controls speech. It also affects her memory. Seven years after moving into her new office, she says she still requires GPS to get to work from her home.

'My brain just can't make those kind of new memories,' she explains.

For a drug-outreach worker, Andrea looks very glamorous, dressed in a designer black turtleneck jumper and jeans. She says that she's always enjoyed expensive things.

Indeed, before ice, Andrea's life must have seemed like the stuff of fairytales to anyone looking in from the outside. As a teenager, she showed a talent for acting and picked up roles in a couple of TV shows before she landed a part that required her to fly to Los Angeles. The burgeoning young starlet fell in love with a dashing (and rich) older man who swept her off her feet. Five years later, she was married with two kids, living in a huge house in the suburbs and driving a Mercedes convertible.

'But it wasn't a fairytale,' she says. Andrea's marriage was difficult but she stuck it out for the sake of her kids. She stayed for nearly ten years until finally, when her youngest child left for university, she walked out.

At first, her newfound freedom was exhilarating. She was not quite forty, and she felt like the glamorous, vivacious actress she had once been. After raising her children, she says that she felt like she was suddenly being offered a second chance at life and love.

'I did it all,' she laughs. 'I'd raised my kids and left my husband. I felt like I'd finished my responsibilities. And then I met this really handsome man . . . you know, I just thought, "Wow".'

But her new Prince Charming had a bit of a wild streak, and a penchant for expensive restaurants, hotels and big nights out. Having spent the best part of her twenties and thirties raising children, Andrea was happy to let her hair down for once and she threw herself into it.

'But when he offered me the pipe, I just said, "Oh no, mate, I don't do drugs."'

She'd never even smoked a joint before that. Drugs had passed her by while she was being a mum in the suburbs. She liked a glass of wine (although not anymore, because the damage ice did to her kidneys means she can't drink now) but her reaction to being offered ice was to say 'no'.

'He said to trust him. He said it would just help me to relax, that it's no big deal.'

She had no idea what a big deal it was.

Andrea describes her first hit on a pipe as 'delicious'. Many addicts describe that first hit with memorable adjectives; I've heard 'delectable', 'sweet' and 'unforgettable'. For Andrea, it started the ball rolling—a ball that would grow into a boulder and smash her whole life to pieces.

'When the devil comes for you, he doesn't come with horns and a tail,' she says. 'No, it's all shining and beautiful and he offers you the world.'

In a $3000-a-night hotel room, the devil came for her. She admits now that she was stupid and naive, but the little glass pipe being offered to her looked so innocent. Andrea says that, ironically, one of the memories that ice hasn't destroyed is her first time. That one she retains in meticulous detail.

Her descent into addiction followed from there. Within three months, she was using five hundred dollars' worth of meth every day. To fund her use, she maxed out the mortgage on her house and sold all her jewellery as well as her Mercedes. When the money ran out, the bank foreclosed on the house and Andrea found herself out on the street. She started selling drugs to pay for her own.

'It's not like you start out thinking, "I wanna become a dealer",' she remembers. 'It doesn't work like that.'

It's hard for me to reconcile the well-dressed, articulate woman sitting in front of me with the shell of a human being she describes herself as back then, lost in the streets, picking up cigarette butts. But while it's hard to imagine how Andrea ever became an addict, it's even harder to imagine how she stopped being one.

Andrea said she became heavily psychotic. Her use had become cyclical—ten days of using, not sleeping, followed by a crash, sleeping for four days, before waking to replay the cycle again. She describes it as living in a prison cell from which she couldn't escape. She would wake up in flophouses which she describes now as how she always imagined hell would look—people everywhere having sex, open prostitution, drugs and guns on display. This was now how Andrea was living her life.

'It was just dark and so horrific, you know?' she says about that world, one she'd hitherto only ever seen in movies. 'You think, "Oh, I won't do that", but then things happen and you go, "Oh, well, I guess it's not that bad if everyone else is doing it."'

Then Andrea had what she describes as a near-death experience. After a particularly intense session, she crashed out. The people she'd been getting high with thought she'd had an overdose. She woke up four days later and ran outside into the street screaming. She says it was the first time she'd been outdoors for weeks but standing there in the road, barely dressed and barely alive, she had what she describes as an 'encounter with God'.

'I started to hear an audible voice which told me to get on a plane, and I had exactly the amount of money that I needed to get the ticket.'

When the plane landed, Andrea went directly home to knock on her mother's front door. She weighed 40 kilos, her hair was falling out and her gums were bleeding from open sores. Her appearance had changed so much that, at first, her mother didn't recognise her.

'I said, "Mum,"' Andrea says. 'And she goes, "Who are you?" I said, "Mum, it's me." And she just stepped back, crying.'

I feel nothing but compassion hearing Andrea talk about this moment. How heartbroken her mother must have been to see her daughter standing there so broken and vulnerable. Yet there's also something hopeful about it. Andrea was demonstrating that she had reached rock bottom but was ready to start rebuilding.

Indeed, that was the moment that Andrea began reconstructing her life, reconnecting with the daughters she hadn't seen for two years and with the woman she had been before she started using meth. She adhered to a program of strict abstinence and prayer, taking one day at a time, putting her past further and further behind her.

Andrea's story may sound tragic, but it is also familiar. What is unusual is the length of time since her epiphany. The ice epidemic in Australia began in earnest only ten years ago. So finding users who consumed ice on the scale that Andrea did and who aren't still using, or dead, is very rare. Andrea's neurologist wants to include her in a paper he's writing because there are so few case studies like hers.

I wonder why she's different. How has she managed to quit and stay quit when so many have failed?

'That's because it is difficult,' she says. 'One, to get out of the mess, and two, to rebuild yourself, to rewire your brain. I had a lot of spiritual help because God came into my life and told me I could start again.'

And that's what she did. She started again. She drew a line in the sand that marked the past and has stayed on the right side of it ever since. She admits that the cravings still come knocking at her door but she remains clean, throwing her energy into helping others to do the same.

Her charity, the AAIC, is a privately run nonprofit that she operates to raise public awareness of the dangers of ice and to help people to 'break free from the cycles of addiction'. Its initiatives range from education in schools to the provision of 'lived-experience buddies' to assist people struggling with ice use.

The person responsible for coordinating the AAIC's buddy program is Andrea's colleague Jeff. Jeff is stocky and heavily tattooed, with a trucker hat perched on the top of a head of thick black hair. He shifts uneasily in his chair as he talks and I notice a visible tic that he works hard to mask.

When Andrea announces that she has to go out for a while, Jeff offers to talk to me about his work at the AAIC. He explains how he recruits and trains the buddies who hold the hands of people who come to AAIC for help, many of whom, he says, are fresh out of rehab and struggling to adjust to life on the outside again. I wonder how someone gets into this line of work.

'I've been inside ten times. The last time was for breaking and entering a house and wounding with a dangerous weapon,' he says, pushing his glasses up his nose and shifting again in his chair with a heavy sigh.

He recalls the rest of that fateful night when he broke into his meth dealer's house with a knife and stabbed him twice before making off with his drugs and cash. Jeff says it was 'lucky' that the guy survived—his survival reduced Jeff's sentence from life to three years. He shrugs off the experience as simply 'part and parcel of being an addict'.

When he got to jail, Jeff says he found himself sharing a cell with a man he'd been in a fight with when they'd been in a junior offenders' institution aged fifteen. That seems to be the story of Jeff's life: in and out of correctional facilities, bumping into the same career criminals—guys who, like him, had violent pasts and significant substance abuse issues. It was when his new cellmate pulled out a bag of ice and started to shoot up that Jeff says he saw the light.

'I'd got to the point where I was just done,' he says.

To Jeff's credit, he sought help on the inside and started to get clean. For him, that meant discovering a religious faith, and so he started to pray. When he prayed, he discovered that the anxiety he was feeling went away, so he prayed more. Pretty soon, he was a committed Christian.

'I'd always believed in a higher power than myself,' he says, 'but something was missing.'

Jeff says that finding the missing elements of stories is something that has always fascinated him. I sit up when he tells me, with no irony, that he believes the earth is flat. His logic is that if the earth were spinning faster than the speed of sound, and then spinning several hundred times faster than that around the sun, 'all the oxygen would get sucked out into space'.

This isn't a physics book, but when I suggest to Jeff that maybe he read one, in particular one about how gravity works, he laughs.

'So how do rockets burn in space if there's no oxygen out there?' he asks, as though he was keeping that killer question up his sleeve for this exact moment.

'I think they carry liquid oxygen on board, no?' I offer.

Jeff doesn't make a counter-argument. He merely waves me away dismissively. 'Yeah, you probably think we've been to the moon,' he says with a flourish.

It's patently absurd, but according to Jeff, Warren Buffett is a Satan worshipper, Hillary Clinton is a paedophile, and billionaires are responsible for abducting millions of children every year.

'I think the reason that these transgenders are killing themselves is 'cos they cut their balls off so they can't regulate without chemicals in their body,' he says, before he adds, 'and it all leads to one place. It's the fucking Jews.'

He admits that he has been prescribed antipsychotic meds by his doctor but that he prefers not to take them. Another of his theories is that medical malpractice is the third-highest cause of death in Australia. Doctors are also part of the New World Order that he fears so much. Instead, Jeff prefers to self-medicate with marijuana, proscribed by the Narcotics Anonymous twelve-step program but the use of which he shrugs off.

'Each to his own,' he laughs.

I think it must be both exhausting and terrifying being Jeff, not being able to trust the state, the medical profession or science. Or at least it must have been before he found God.

'God just keeps putting me everywhere I need to be,' he says.

He says that God told him to volunteer in a homeless shelter when he got out of jail. That's where he heard about the local Narcotics Anonymous meeting, which is where he met Andrea and found out about the AAIC.

Narcotics Anonymous (NA) is a community-based recovery program for people who express a desire to live a drug-free life. There are no membership fees, so groups have to support themselves, which often just means finding a space to meet and the cost of tea and biscuits. NA is now a truly global organisation that operates in forty-nine different languages and is open to all.

Although NA purports to not be allied with any religion, it does contain a spiritual element. The twelve-step program requires members to accept that a 'Power greater than ourselves could restore us to sanity' and admit that they are 'ready to have God remove all these defects of character' and 'remove our shortcomings'. At Jeff's meetings, he says a Christian pastor or chaplain usually reads to them from the Bible or offers a sermon.

Jeff says that the twelve steps told him not only who God was but how to find him. Now he believes that he's doing God's work, committed to the AAIC and helping Andrea to spread the word about the harmful effects of ice in their community.

A large part of the AAIC's work is helping those who are ready to quit to stay off ice. Jeff says that when someone has reached their low point or rock bottom and is ready to ask for help then he's there to offer it. Because he has thirty years of addiction behind him, that life experience qualifies him to know how to speak to addicts in a way they understand, and even to know what is the best form for that help to take. That might include knowing which rehab facility is best suited to the individual or which buddy to assign to them for support. Jeff's role seems crucial to an individual's success in getting sober.

Meanwhile, Jeff is still dealing with his own addictive past. He says that the eighth and ninth steps of the program are the ones he thinks about the most—the ones that relate to confronting the sins of one's past and making amends to those who may have been harmed along the way. It seems to me that in Jeff's case, that's a pretty long list, but he says that being a born-again Christian helps absolve him of responsibility.

'It is done,' he says. 'We're washed clean and so we just move on.'

Of course, like nearly every problematic user I've met on this journey, Jeff has his own history of personal trauma: an abusive stepfather, who ostracised and excluded him from the family home. Young Jeff found comfort in drug use, and associations with gangs and crime quickly followed.

———

A week later, I get a very, very long email from Luke. It's unlike him. In our previous correspondence, he's always been economical with words, clear and concise, but this message is rambling, at times incoherent. It sets alarm bells ringing, and I anticipate the worst. I message back and immediately he replies again to confirm my suspicions— he's out of rehab, back in Brisbane, living in a hostel, using meth again. My heart sinks.

Luke's hostel is bright yellow. It was once a back-packers' spot, somewhere that travellers would stop off for a couple of days if they were travelling along the coast. It's the kind of place that I would have stayed at in my twenties. It looks fun, somewhere to meet fellow travel-lers, a base to explore the city and maybe make some new friends. However, when I arrive to meet Luke, it doesn't take long for that impression to change.

There's a group of three men and two women sitting in plastic chairs out the front of the hostel. A couple of them are young, mid-twenties, but these guys aren't backpackers. They look up from their conversation as I approach. One is smoking a joint; another has a box of beers tucked under the chair next to his feet. I detect no animosity but still, there's a distance, a sort of disconnectedness about how they engage with me when I ask if they know where I can find Luke.

The youngest of the group, a tall, rakish young man with a pubic moustache, unfolds himself from his chair and invites me to follow him. He greets me with a cold, damp handshake and introduces himself as Craig. Craig says that he and Luke share a room but that I'll need his key to get inside. I follow him through a security door and find Luke lying on the bottom bunk in a dark dorm room.

The room smells acrid, a blend of men's sweat and marijuana. Another man is snoring on a bed in the corner, not stirring as Luke gets up to welcome me. Although we've only ever met online before, I feel as though we've struck up enough of a rapport to offer him a hug. His body feels warm and clammy, and his frame feels firmer, more athletic than I'd imagined. Later, he'll explain that he got kicked out of rehab for injecting testosterone, something he does semi-regularly to help build muscle.

Luke takes me outside and introduces me to the gang. As well as Craig with the moustache, who turns out to be the local dealer, there's Sally who scribbles constantly into the margins of an old Bible; Dave with the beers, whose favourite topic of conversation is the various agencies who are following him; and Carl, who is almost inappropriately enthusiastic about everything and offers to make me a cup of tea every five minutes. All of them, including Luke, are high on ice.

For a while, I sit with the group, trying to keep up with the conversation, starting to see how ice affects the way that they communicate with each other. Five people are having a conversation but everyone seems quite dissociated, at times listening to each other, at other times not, so that sometimes it feels like multiple conversations are happening at once, only coming together for fleeting moments. Suddenly, Craig turns to me and asks what my book is about.

'Ice,' I say.

Sally jumps in. 'Ice is the drug of choice here. Everything else too, but mainly ice.'

Craig seems to agree. 'You could write a bestseller if you wrote about your experiences around here, but be careful with all the crew like us that are doing it tough.'

Then, out of nowhere, Dave throws in a curveball. 'I love Trump. He's as corrupt as everybody else but 'cos of what he did over Covid, he gets my vote.'

'Nobody knows the law,' Carl says, with a knowing smile.

Sally seems to agree. 'If you don't sign something then you're not liable. Did we sign every law? No, we didn't, so we're not liable.'

Dave nods. 'Trump never did the vaccine either. Not the one they're giving people now.'

'Some people don't even meet their mum and dad,' Sally continues.

I'm starting to feel lost.

'We're just waiting for President Trump to return,' Dave says pointedly to me, but before I can respond, Carl touches my arm.

'Did you believe in the Queen?' he asks.

'There's people that have been cut out of their parents' guts and then they didn't give a shit about their own kids.' Sally is now shouting to be heard over the others.

'She'd been dead for years,' Carl says, determined not to be shut down by Sally. 'Several years before they publicised it.'

'Can we not talk about death?' Craig replies.

I'm surprised he's listening.

Sally sighs. 'I'm suicidal. But I do love my mum and dad.'

Craig turns back to me again. 'Be careful of the blokes here. If they get upset, that's when you just walk away and go, "Oh, I'm going to go and get a fucking drink, see you in a little while."'

Sally lights a cigarette. 'My dad taught me how to ride a bike.'

'Don't you steal my bike!' Dave says to her with a laugh.

'Don't steal my heart, mate,' Sally replies with a smile.

'My heart's been broken in so many different places,' Dave says.

'Just placate 'em,' Craig says. He's looking at me with a frightening intensity now. 'Because if you hit 'em and you bust your skin . . . A lot of these cunts around here got hep C and fucking who knows what.'

'Hep C?' Dave asks.

'That's what did for the Queen,' Carl replies.

'No, it was her heart,' Dave says solemnly.

Everybody nods in agreement and the conversation goes quiet again.

I suggest to Luke that we take a walk. I want to talk to him privately about why he thinks he sabotaged his rehab by injecting testosterone. He grumbles about the lack of common ground with the people who were supervising him. He says that none of the nurses, the counsellors or the doctors had any lived experience of drug use, or at least not one they were ready to share. He says that it's hard to explain to someone who's never used drugs how nothing in the whole world will ever feel as good as drugs do.

I think back to the enthusiasm that Luke showed a couple of months ago, how he spoke so confidently about getting off drugs and back to writing. There's a lie in there somewhere but I can't quite put my finger on where it is. I'm sure Luke wasn't lying when he said it and I even doubt that he was lying to himself. On the contrary, I think he meant every word when he spoke about completing the program and the book, but all that seems patently untrue now. So was it a lie?

The sad truth is that rehab is hard. More than 35 per cent of people who enter rehab fail to complete it successfully, and many more of those who do complete it end up using again. Luke and his mates at the hostel have all given it a go and ended up back at square one.

Epidemiologist Rebecca McKetin estimates that there could be as many as 350,000 problematic or dependent ice users in Australia today. That's people who use at least once a week.

'Particularly with meth, when people are intoxicated, they're still quite functional, which masks problems, and gives people a sense of well-being and competence,' she says. 'So they think they're often doing quite fine when other people might not see it that way. And they want to keep going.'

That means that a considerable number of those 350,000 people aren't ready to even ask for help yet, never mind going into rehab. Even after they lose their job, get a warning from their doctor or start seeing things that aren't there, they can be in denial for a considerable period. It's not until the wheels come well and truly off—like Mark getting caught with a loaded firearm in the back of his car, or Shawnee seeing men in trenchcoats—that rehab becomes a viable option in the mind of a dependent user.

————

'I was a doctor, I'm still a doctor,' says Sam the psychiatrist.

Sam has asked that we meet at a roadside store in a regional town, a couple of hours west of Brisbane. I assume that's because he doesn't want to bump into anyone who might ask questions about what he's doing talking to me. Sam's experience of meth use is something that he's still learning to talk about and, understandably, he still fears the consequences of being stigmatised as a meth user or even a former meth user when he's part of the medical profession.

He's still a young man, mid-thirties, slight but athletically built with short-cropped red hair. He's chosen to wear a pair of wraparound reflective sunglasses today so I can't see his eyes. He reminds me a little of Bono from U2.

Sam explains how he's been putting his life together after everything went down the drain. Before he ever took meth, he was a practising psychiatrist who saved his money in a carefully managed investment fund. He says that he lived a 'very cautious life', and prioritised work and his career, although he adds that he did 'dabble' in opioid use for over a decade.

But when Sam decided to give meth a go, everything changed and his life quickly began to spiral. A year later, he was unemployed and had spent fifty grand of his life savings plus the hundred grand he'd earned that year on ice. All his money gone on meth, most of which he says got flushed down the toilet in paranoia, only to be replaced again the next day.

'I'd get high and just go and buy shit on the internet,' he says. 'I had a whole living room just full of crap. No idea what was in there. It was all brand new. Most of it never came out of the box.'

His social circle changed drastically. He went from hanging out with other medical professionals who occasionally used recreational drugs, to hanging out with his dealer, driving him around, getting involved with his criminal enterprise in places where he was regularly seeing guns and large quantities of drugs.

'I was an upper-middle-class white kid from the suburbs in a small coastal town. It's not like I came from the block.' He still looks a little baffled about it all. 'I think they were people who were living in chaos and that chaos started to have a rewarding appeal to it. I'd become conditioned to seek it out.'

Until, inevitably, Sam got arrested.

'I hadn't slept for days and days and days, then I packed all of my possessions into the car and just drove around trying to avoid some people I thought were coming to get me. I ran my car into an embankment and when the police arrived, I had a bunch of drugs on me in the car.'

Even on bail, he found it hard to modify his behaviour as his ice use had become so habitual. He narrowly avoided arrest another couple of times. It was only when a family member flew in from overseas to stage an intervention and physically drag him out of his situation that things changed. Sam was lucky. He had a family with sufficient resources to book him into a rehab facility in a different city, away from the triggers that were entrenched in his habitual patterns of use.

He's been clean ever since but it still took three years to convince the Medical Board that he was okay to return to work. Maybe that goes some way to show how the stigma involved in meth applies even within the medical community. If Sam had been convicted of drink driving, he'd have been back and registered again a lot sooner.

'Even though it was all three years ago,' he says, 'it's been a three-year process of being constantly assessed whether I'm a risk to the public.'

He just got his registration back, and will resume practising psychiatry in the next month.

I'm interested to hear Sam's perspective on my experience over the last couple of weeks of spending time with users up in Brisbane and on the Gold Coast who have shown signs of psychosis. One thing I have questioned is, with these problematic users, which is the chicken and which is the egg? There seems to be quite a considerable proclivity for conspiracy theories among those with even mildly psychotic behaviours, so I've started to wonder if the people who are exhibiting paranoia and delusional behaviour are particularly vulnerable to meth, or whether those kinds of paranoid delusions are more a symptom of doing meth. Which comes first?

'I think from my perspective it can be a combination of both,' Sam says, taking a swig of his coffee, the only stimulant he still partakes in these days. 'Certainly in some people, it's going to go one way or the other, but just from my background and my personal experience of having psychosis frequently while using meth, at least in the mental health field we view that as a common side effect.'

Sam says that as a psychiatrist treating patients with schizophrenia, psychosis in bipolar disorder or psychosis in depression, he routinely prescribes drugs that block dopamine receptors. On the other hand, meth stimulates the body to release vast quantities of dopamine, which then floods your brain.

'So taking meth is like taking the opposite of an anti-psychotic,' he says. 'It certainly seems far more common to see psychosis as a result of meth use than from any of the other drugs commonly in use, and that's because of the way it works directly by releasing dopamine.'

This raises a problem for those who argue that meth should be treated in the same way as all other drugs. Most other recreational drugs give you pleasure via dopamine release, which is what makes them feel rewarding, but that's a secondary effect. Meth increases the release of dopamine while simultaneously slowing down dopamine uptake in the brain, which means it remains active for far longer than other drugs, and is why there's a significantly higher risk of psychosis with meth use. Then you throw in a few days of sleep deprivation on top of that—which, as anyone who's experienced jet lag will tell you, makes you feel a little unhinged—and you're on your way to a psychotic episode.

Another unique characteristic of meth use, especially for problematic users, is that staying awake for twenty-four hours or more at a time is common. In that case, you can multiply these effects exponentially until the lack of sleep causes profound changes in perception and cognition.

'If you've combined that inevitable sleep deprivation with a high dose of meth or protracted meth use, then you've got the perfect recipe for psychosis,' Sam says.

I wonder if that's part of the attraction. As perverse as it sounds, is deliberately and wilfully soliciting a feeling of psychosis part of the escapism that makes the drug attractive to certain people?

'It is,' Sam nods, 'and perhaps not just the dissociation from the reality around you, which often for people with problematic use isn't very pleasant. The objective reality of their existence can often be pretty messy and have a lot of downsides to it. So taking a little break from that internally and not having to be as aware of that might be nice.'

But Sam also believes that there's something even more profound than simple escapism.

'A lot of meth-induced delusions are ego-driven—the police are watching me, the FBI's watching me, I'm being followed. It gives you a sense of importance.'

This is not something I've heard before but it makes a lot of sense. If you don't identify with social norms or you don't feel like you've got a position in society that satisfies your ego, which a lot of meth users do not, then imagining that you are the focus of an investigation could fill a need.

So many of the users that I have spoken with have experienced (or have been in the middle of) a psychosis that included feelings of being followed or surveilled. It makes sense that the brain, to overcome feelings of being alone or ignored by society, conjures up a narrative that puts the user front and centre in the action. It's objectively paranoiac to think that the CIA are after you, but to a delusional mind, it might feel quite exciting. The problem is that those exciting feelings start to become quite exhausting after a couple of nights without sleep.

I feel like the picture that Sam is painting of meth is quite a bleak one, especially in terms of reducing harm and working towards the destigmatisation of drugs in society. Objectively, Sam believes that meth is riskier than other drugs. He has written as much for the nonprofit charity Unharm. He argues that we risk missing an opportunity to engage in an open and honest debate about other drugs as long as we continue to deny that meth is different.

In Sam's view, it is down to the way meth works: the direct reinforcement of behaviour associated with dopamine release, the activation of the reward centre that convinces you that pretty much anything you are doing you are doing better, and you enjoy more, when you're using meth.

And that goes for work too—another area where meth differs. There are cases all over Australia and Asia of people using meth at work. That's fairly unique with drugs—most people would struggle to take heroin or MDMA before work. Some people work to pay for their gear and use the gear to enjoy the work. I know journalists who have fallen into this pattern. You can repeat the cycle for a while until it catches up to you. You'll enjoy the work more. You'll think you're doing it better; you probably aren't, but you'll think you are.

I wonder how Sam is going to deal with having patients who are experiencing the same thing that he went through.

'I had a very non-judgemental approach before because I'd grown up around some drug use, but even more so now as I've been there myself. Now I get it. I understand how disempowering it feels to be dragged into a hospital when you don't think you need to be there and don't want to be there.'

At the end of the day, many users know more about the drugs they're taking than the doctors examining them do. Sam says that he's heard colleagues telling patients not to buy cannabis on the street because somebody might have put meth in it.

This is clearly bogus. Why would somebody take a $20-per-gram drug like cannabis and cut it with a $500-per-gram stimulant like meth? Not only is it bad economics but it would give the user the opposite experience of what they were looking for. It's an absurd concept, and it's worrying that a frontline doctor might believe it to be true.

The danger is that if a user knows this isn't true, they will suspect that the doctor doesn't know what they're talking about, and the user will then not listen to any good advice the doctor might impart. Even if everything that comes out of the doctor's mouth after that ridiculous thing is perfectly good, perfectly reasonable advice, they've already lost all credibility in the eyes of the user.

I wonder what Sam makes of the TV advert in which the meth user smashes the ER room to shreds. How does it tally with his experience of working in an actual psychiatric unit?

'As a psychiatrist, I have to admit people to hospital in those states. It does happen,' he says. 'But users know that it's not always true, so they ignore all of it. You end up not knowing what information the government's giving you about risk and harm that is true, and what is just fear-based crap.'

This seems like a perfect case of where Sam's lived experience can dovetail with his medical expertise. He's been there, he's done it, and he can speak to it credibly. He knows enough, as a former user, for example, to see that the official messaging around methamphetamine needs to be very different from the messaging around cannabis. Currently, the two don't look that different but it's not true that they present the same risks to users. And drug users aren't stupid. You can't convince users to take steps to reduce those risks if you are pretending these things are all the same, and all present the same level of danger.

'As a user, you're always looking for that one little piece of ridiculousness so you can go, "This person has no idea what they're talking about", just to shut it down entirely and not listen to any of it,' Sam says.

The problem with misinformed messaging is the same as the scare-tactic adverts on the TV. Anyone who's used drugs without turning into the Incredible Hulk, without headbutting a doctor or hurling a chair at a window, is at risk of dismissing the advert as hyperbolic and ignoring the message altogether.

If the government's telling you that the first time you take MDMA, your brain's going to explode from water or you're going to go nuts and beat your mum up, but every time you've gone out to a festival since you were twelve years old, you've seen 50,000 people taking drugs without any of that going on, then you're going to question the messaging. And if you lose faith in all the messaging, then when you get some messaging around a drug that puts you at an objectively higher risk of dependence, of harmful outcomes or of abuse, the danger is that you will dismiss that too.

That's why it's good that we're seeing more peer-based workers included in mental health teams and treatment teams. People with that lived experience are coming in and being able to talk to the patients. But at the same time, it needs to be carefully managed and rigorously applied.

Once you can start educating people about the differences between drugs, you can start providing some education about what you can do and minimise those risks. With meth, that might include messaging around the dangers of injecting, or even of smoking versus taking it orally to slow down the speed at which it hits your system. If you can dissuade users from experiencing that massive initial rush, then you can reduce the dopamine reward that you get from dosing via the needle or the pipe.

Sam agrees. 'If you can get that kind of messaging into people's heads before they're lost in a cycle of addiction, you can still potentially reduce the harms. Once people have already gone down that path then it's a lot harder to start bringing harm-reduction practices into what they do.'

It is often too late. Education isn't going to change people who have fallen foul of haphazard, destructive injecting practices. By that point, the damage is done and something new has to be tried. Rehab and lived-experience counselling could be useful but, again, it needs to be regulated.

I'm as heartened by rehabilitation success stories like Sam's as I am saddened by Luke's remission into addiction again. It's a reminder that every individual case of meth use in Australia has its own prognosis. Among all the stats and figures, it's easy to lose hold of that. If rehabilitation and education in the community are to be part of Australia's multipronged strategy to reduce the societal damage caused by methamphetamine, then policymakers need to get a handle on it because it needs more Sams and fewer Lukes to make it work. And then there's Andrea.

There's no doubt that Andrea's story is inspiring. She is living proof that there is life after meth. She is a unicorn, maybe, but still a living example of someone who has reclaimed sobriety. Her journey is to be marvelled at and could be inspirational to someone keen to put problematic meth use behind them. However, I can't help but question her judgement when it comes to Jeff. While he also has an admirable recovery story, I wonder if a transphobic, antisemitic conspiracy theorist is the best person to entrust with vulnerable people in recovery.

It's clear that there are still not enough regulations in place for the rehab industry, and no specific minimum requirements to govern how private drug-rehabilitation or associated programs are run. Government-funded centres do exist alongside the unregulated private sector, and evidence-based treatment programs are available at low cost to consumers, but waiting lists for these options are long.

The NSW government's Special Commission of Inquiry into the Drug Ice found that up to half a million people each year across Australia need help and seek drug addiction treatment but do not get it. In New South Wales, for example, one in five people seeking addiction treatment must wait up to six months. People experiencing problematic meth use know that they can't wait that long, and families desperate to get help for loved ones increasingly must turn to the private sector.

It's understandably hard for a society to keep throwing money at such an imperfect solution. When even well-run rehab centres have such a high dropout rate, and the number of people relapsing remains frustratingly high, there's a temptation to write it off as not working. But I think that's shortsighted.

Australia needs to ask whether it is getting the most from a system that is so woefully unregulated. Jeff is a perfect example of what you get if you leave things to develop for themselves. There is a valuable place for people with lived experiences to operate in the rehabilitation and educational spaces but more must be done to oversee how they are used within a wider framework.

At a bare minimum, a government-run accreditation system should be considered. Properly run, it would protect users and their families by ensuring that they receive evidence-based treatment, underpinned by best practice, from qualified individuals. That could cover a range of factors including staff vetting and training, evidence-based therapies, and coordination with broader health care services after users leave rehab. It's important to remember there is no 'one size fits all' and, like any other health problem, not every drug-rehabilitation treatment will suit every person. But there should at least be a standardised minimum level of care made available to people who are seeking help. It might take you a few attempts to find the right one but, eventually, we should start to see more people like Sam emerging, people who can be rehabilitated back into society to start contributing again.

But rehab can't work on its own. It needs to be part of the solution, one that concerns itself rightly with reducing the demand for drugs within Australian society among those who have already begun using. Beyond rehab, we need to look at the issue of how to limit the supply of drugs at source, and that means investigating further how they are finding their way to users in the first place. To do that, we need to take a look at how the law enforcement community can align itself with harm-reduction strategies, and how, after accepting defeat, a society can come up with an entirely new approach.

10

LAW AND DISORDER

The sky is a cloudless powder-blue as I pull off the main highway before the Gold Coast and head against the flow of morning peak-hour traffic into Southport. The port that was established 150 years ago now feels like a middle-class suburb of the Gold Coast, with shopping centres, high-rise office blocks and properties that overlook the pretty Broadwater and beyond to the beach.

Tucked into the armpit of one of Southport's more salubrious residential postcodes is a homeless outreach shelter that operates as a kind of soup kitchen, doling out a free lunch and a cup of tea to rough sleepers, many of whom bedded down last night in their cars in one of the local car parks. The shelter is an important hub for this community, a place for them to hang out and socialise with each other. It's also a place for people looking to score drugs to meet Vix.

Remember Vix? She was the dealer who introduced me to Chris, the shake-and-bake cook from chapter one. When I get to the shelter, I find her enjoying a cup of tea, surrounded by people, sitting at long trestle tables enjoying their lunch. She suggests we step outside into the morning sunshine, and while she peddles small quantities of ice to other homeless people, she talks very openly to me about her experiences. It's pretty obvious that she is well known and well liked.

I'm interested to hear how Vix, a fifty-something-year-old woman, has ended up dealing drugs, while staying clear of the kind of psychosis or mental health issues that I've seen in so many other users.

She explains that it was her ex-partner who first introduced her to ice about four years ago during what she describes as a toxic relationship. She had once been a very heavy drinker but at the time she met the guy, she'd been sober for three years. Her meth use quickly escalated but she caught it before it got out of hand. Despite her problematic history with alcohol, she says she's always been able to keep on top of her ice use.

'A lot of people take ice and think they're addicted. But it's all about your mentality, I find. I've seen people get off it, lots of people use it recreationally on the weekends. I've done addiction, I'm not going to do it again,' she says.

Vix says that she did rehab several times for her drinking and she spent countless hours in therapy rooms. But the sharp-stop approach never worked for her, while the rehab ethos of 'once an addict, always an addict' offered her no hope. In the same way that alcohol and drugs rewired her brain, she believes that only by changing her mentality again did she change her outcome. I wonder how that works, how she manages to keep her use under control when so many seem incapable of doing so.

'I make sure I take breaks. I take days, weeks, months off,' she explains. 'I make sure I treat myself better. I eat, sleep and drink. I don't do those things when I'm on it.'

Vix says that people like her—homeless people going through the worst time of their lives—are no different from anyone else in society facing a difficult situation. At those times, don't we all look for something to make us feel good, something that can help pick us up? Whether it's chocolate, coffee, a trip to the cinema or a glass of wine, whatever makes you feel better about yourself is what gets you through those times.

But of course, unlike those things, ice is illegal, which is where Vix's relationship with it does become problematic.

'I used to sell more, maybe an ounce in a day,' she says. 'Less now, and not all in points. A lot of my customers are in work so they can afford to buy more.'

The economics of her business is interesting. She explains that she can pick up an ounce (28 grams) of 'pure' ice for around $6000 from her dealer, a guy who she says, like Chris, was once a cook and still has good connections. Because the quality is so high, she can cut the ounce 3:1 with MSM.

Meth is often cut with MSM, a popular supplement available at health food stores, often used by gym bros after working out. It looks like ice and has a similar boiling point so that when you burn it in a pipe, it's hard to tell the difference. MSM is cheap to buy, so adding it to ice can increase your profit margins considerably.

'People don't realise, even when they put it in a pipe. It looks just the same,' she says.

After cutting it down, Vix can turn an ounce into 40 grams, which her biggest customers pick up in eight balls (3.5 grams) at $1000 each, or grams at $500. She says that she prefers to keep dealing points (0.1 grams) to a minimum but that when she does, she can charge $60 or $70. When all is said and done, her $6000 outlay can yield double that.

I wonder whether she ever feels vulnerable, dealing drugs as a woman, having that kind of cash passing through her hands. She would make a juicy target for any would-be criminal.

'As a chick on your own, you've got to have some backup,' she says. 'But you don't want to have to call on them too often. Better to keep that trouble from your door in the first place.'

She puts her success at doing exactly that down to keeping a low profile and never talking about anything that could get her associates in trouble. When I ask her if that means bikie gangs, she shrugs. 'Some have associations with bikie gangs, but others don't.'

Vix is referring to the guy who's been watching us the whole time that we've been talking. He's a 6-foot, unshaven, sinewy guy with tattoos on his knuckles—BORIS on the left hand, JULES on the other—keeping an eye on us from the other side of the yard. Vix calls him over and introduces him as Rich.

As Rich shakes my hand with Jules, I see him up close, and it's clear that he's another rough sleeper. His hand feels rough, and even though he's had a shower and a cup of coffee, I can still detect a whiff of last night's booze on his breath. Rich is Vix's muscle, the guy who will step in when needed to handle any trouble that might come her way. His qualifications for such a position seem to have been earned over a lifetime that has been characterised by violence and time in jail.

Rich tells me that two of his cousins are 'patched' members of the Gypsy Jokers, a motorcycle gang, in South Australia, and that he has another cousin who is a lifetime member of the Western Australian chapter. Rich himself has never been patched—never officially made a member—but still had longstanding associations with the gang.

Over the last two decades, Rich has been in and out of jail frequently, doing muscle jobs over the years for the gang on the inside and out. He's bashed non-payers, collected debts, delivered rough justice to people who were deemed to have crossed the line. He says he once torched a man's house for non-payment of a drug debt and recently spent two years inside for bashing his uncle so badly that he had to be rushed to the hospital for surgery. Rich was already on parole for a prior assault and so he went straight back into the clink.

Since he last got out, three weeks ago, Rich says he's been sleeping in his car. His wife left him a year ago and moved with their kids to Southport. Rich got kicked out of his last house for not paying the rent and so now his car is his home, parked around the corner from his ex-wife's new apartment, hoping that she'll allow him to see his sons again soon.

In the meantime, Rich is operating as Vix's minder, keeping an eye on her while she's dealing ice around Southport. He says that they both operate independently, free of any association with the Gypsy Jokers, which is unusual. Bikie gangs are not known to be very agreeable to people leaving. Yet somehow, Rich got a pass which he says was granted in return for a final display of loyalty.

Before starting his last stint inside, Rich went to his boss and asked for permission to leave. He said that request was granted in return for him delivering a message to an individual who had crossed the gang and was serving time in the same prison. Rich stabbed the man twice in the backside. He was never identified as the assailant, nobody ever 'dobbed', but the important people knew that he was prepared to do whatever they asked. And for that, his request was granted.

'They expect everyone to rob them,' he says. 'Especially if you're a knock-along guy or a tag-along or a nom, but I never robbed anyone. I was always loyal and so I had a good name.'

Rich leveraged that good name to get out of the gang. He was lucky. I've read horror stories of guys wanting to quit their memberships who have had their legs broken, their heads smashed in or worse. Rich describes once being part of a 'run the gauntlet' exercise where a gang member who wanted to get out had to pass along a tunnel of guys who beat him with bats. The guy was eventually dragged out unconscious and spent a long period in hospital as the price for his freedom.

This process is clearly barbaric and speaks very well to the violence and brutality of the bikie gangs. Not only are these boys' clubs operating as mafias, knee-deep in prostitution, racketeering and drug distribution, but they continue to intimidate the society that they depend upon.

I wonder if Rich has had to use his fists since he started working for Vix. 'Nah,' he laughs. 'Boris and Jules have had a quiet few weeks.'

———

From the Australian Criminal Intelligence Commission data available for 2019–20, it's clear that the focus of law enforcement is still to target users of meth. Nationally, there were 43,428 arrests of amphetamine users made in the period, compared to just 5504 arrests of amphetamine suppliers. So only around one in ten arrests for amphetamines are of dealers.

If we look at what was seized during those arrests, we begin to get a broader view of what is going on. State police made 37,235 amphetamine seizures totalling 2.8 tonnes, an average of about 76 grams per seizure. Comparing that rate with AFP seizures is quite striking because the AFP seizure amount is so much higher (1969 seizures, totalling 10 tonnes), averaging more than 5 kilos per seizure.

Also, and I think this is just as relevant, the purity levels of the meth discovered are pretty similar no matter who found them. For example, the NSW Police seized meth with a median purity level of 77.5 per cent, while the AFP's median purity rate for NSW seizures was 77.1 per cent.

What do all those stats mean?

I think they describe a clear narrative where users and small-time dealers are being targeted by state police with very little impact on the overall supply, while larger dealers and distributors, picked up by the radar of the AFP, are turning up much bigger wins.

The importance of large-scale supply reduction can be seen by looking at the US experience. It's easy to think the efforts of the AFP and Australian Border Force are pointless because the price of meth remains stable, but consider what would happen were they not there, stopping meth at the border. In the US, where the meth market is served by labs in Mexico—a country in which labs have popped up in their hundreds over the last decade—the price of meth has fallen to less than US$2000 per kilogram, a 90 per cent drop from a decade earlier. Were such a thing to happen in the Australian market, use would likely increase too.

The data in Australia also show that the meth hitting the streets in 2019–20 was pretty much the same as the meth that was produced at scale, which we know is of higher purity. So shake-and-bake meth, which we know has a lower purity, doesn't look like it is diluting the overall supply, which means the volume must not be significant.

The final piece in this puzzle is found in the bottom line. What are Australian taxpayers doling out to support these two different strategies? And, crucially, which one is producing better value for money?

Estimating Australia's annual drug law enforcement expenditure is a difficult and inexact science. For example, how can you work out exactly what proportion of the money spent tackling organised crime is for drug law enforcement, given that drugs are just one source of income for gangs? Any estimation is further confounded by the lack of documentation by police services of activity-based time allocation, never mind breaking these numbers down further to know what is spent by states versus federally.

But that said, let's look at some reasonable estimates that have been attempted.

A report conducted by the team at the Drug Policy Modelling Program at the University of New South Wales estimated that in 2009–10 Australian drug law enforcement activities cost just over $1 billion. This total figure included police services, judicial resources, legal expenses, corrective services, the AFP and the Australian Border Force. The report made some reasonable assumptions to further break down the total and produce estimates that the AFP share of this pie earmarked for drug-related investigations was approximately $90 million, while the total state/territory policing budget dedicated to drug enforcement was $388 million.

I'm going to assume that the proportion spent on meth-related drug enforcement in the state police versus the proportion spent in the AFP is broadly similar. In which case, it's the ratios that matter—the state cops are spending more than four times as much money on policing drugs in Australia as the AFP.

And let's remember that despite spending four times as much money, the state police are seizing significantly less than the AFP. In other words, in terms of meth seizures that stop meth from hitting the streets of Australia, the AFP is at least fifteen times more effective than the state police, per dollar spent.

I accept that this is a very rough estimate—an educated guess—using the best data available, which itself is less than comprehensive. But the implications, even if I'm half right, are potentially huge. It could be time to radically change our thinking on where money is being spent.

There could be enormous potential to improve Australia's capacity to reduce supply by simply engaging in a sensible debate about spending priorities. The potential for such improvements is important enough to at least expect the Australian government to immediately demand better and more recent data.

It certainly looks coherent. If the average seizure of amphetamines by state police is only 76 grams, then a single tonne seized at the border by the AFP is the equivalent of 13,000 state police seizures. Imagine the hours, the paperwork generated, the lives ruined, even the dollars spent on 13,000 seizures, and you start to understand why tackling drug supply at street level is such a waste of time.

I keep returning to the question of 'What do we want?' If the point of drug law enforcement is to reduce supply, to make it harder for drugs to find their way into our communities and to lock up those who are pushing those drugs onto the streets, then the state police strategy seems to be bad value for money, while the AFP strategy seems to be a better one.

That could have profound implications for how we deal with people like Chris, Vix and Rich.

Admittedly, Chris is a danger to himself and a potential red flag for the local fire station, but the data suggests that people like him—small-time shake-and-bake cooks, operating out of their kitchens—are not the major suppliers of methamphetamine to the community.

Chris supplies Vix, who in turn supplies a handful of users in the Southport area. What is the impact of arresting her and shutting down her supply? By her account, you'll take one ounce of meth off the streets. But for how long? Nearly all the people who Vix supplies are addicts, and they will undoubtedly find another Vix quickly. Addiction doesn't go away because you take a penny-and-dime dealer off the street.

Frankly, targeting Chris and Vix as part of a wider law enforcement strategy seems like a waste of time and money.

Which leaves Rich.

Yes, Rich is a thug but, by his own admission, his talent for extreme violence was only engaged while he was in the service of an organised crime group that was involved with large-scale meth distribution. Since he's been working for Vix, he's become a silent deterrent, there to discourage violence, not provoke it.

If Australia wants different outcomes, then, like Vix, it's going to have to change its attitude.

———

Before Mick Palmer became the commissioner of the Australian Federal Police, he was police commissioner in the Northern Territory. He has one of the most impressive CVs in Australian law enforcement, with a degree in law, an Australian Police Medal and an Order of Australia among his considerable accolades. Now Mick, a tall, lean man with a good head of white hair and piercing blue eyes, has agreed to meet me at a trendy brunch spot in a beachside town near the New South Wales–Queensland border, where he retired after thirty-three years of service.

'It was pretty unforgiving when it comes to drugs,' he remembers about his time in the Northern Territory.

'We were spending a heap of money and police resources and not making any bloody difference, no matter how many people we arrested.'

When it comes to policing in Australia, Mick says the challenges are often not what is going to work best but what can we convince the electorate is going to work. Mick says that in the case of the Northern Territory, the view of drug addicts was 'pretty hardcore'. But when Marshall Perron was elected chief minister of the territory in the late 1980s, Mick decided there was a chance to persuade the new guy that it was time to take a slightly different approach.

He made time to see his new boss and argued that what they were doing wasn't working, that trying to police your way out of prohibition sounded good but that the results proved they weren't achieving their objectives. Even with some of the most effective policing in the Western world, the 'strong on drugs, strong on the users of drugs' strategy wasn't making any difference.

'If we'd been a business, by any measure of success, we'd have gone bust,' he says. 'I said, "We've just got to think of new ways to do business, and if it doesn't work, we change it."'

The new chief minister didn't knock him back, but he did have his reservations.

'He said, "Look, we all know what to do, we just dunno how to get re-elected after we do it,"' Mick remembers.

Mick said that is when he realised that he needed to get involved in challenging the status quo, educating the electorate, and using his impressive credentials as a police officer to lead the debate on how a change of approach could lead to an improvement in outcomes. Mick started presenting his experiences everywhere he could exert influence, something he continues to do into retirement.

'I started doing Rotary Club addresses,' Mick says. 'These guys are all successful business owners. They tend to be Liberal, right wing, and don't have too much sympathy for drug users.'

Mick knew that if he could get Rotary people to change their minds, and ask them to think again about their prejudices, then he could kickstart a wider change of attitude. The people he was talking to were exactly the sort of people who routinely talk to politicians. If he could get them to see that it was time to try something new, that what they were trying now wasn't working, then he had a chance to change the political will to do something about it.

'In every case, without exception, their attitudes were changed,' Mick says. 'They'd come up to me and say things like, "I'd never stopped to think about it from that point of view."'

Many Rotarians were keen to know how they could help, and how they could get involved. It's maybe no surprise that people who were used to getting things done wanted to know how to get involved. Mick was clear that he needed allies—people pushing the debate, clearing the path for others to express their views freely. Even now, Mick feels that senior police officers still don't have the confidence to say what they really think.

'A lot of operational police can see the fallacy and the failure in what they're doing,' he sighs. 'They're locking up kids who are the same age as they are. So there's a lot more understanding at the operational level, but senior management still sometimes feel that they can't express themselves openly in case they lose their jobs.'

I've heard this called post-retirement enlightenment syndrome. Serving officers continue to repeat the party line that all drugs are bad and all drug users must be punished but then the minute they retire from the police force, offering up a more progressive view of drug use. As if by magic, they start to argue that harm reduction should be prioritised and that users are victims of their addiction.

In 2019, the NSW government spent $11 million on a landmark inquiry into crystal methamphetamine addiction in what seemed to many like a tacit admission that whatever they were doing up until that point wasn't working. The report took fourteen months to complete and another two years for the government to respond to. Maybe that was because the commission was scathing about the state's approach to law enforcement in respect of meth, and called for a complete overhaul of a 'tired' justice system, including a move towards decriminalising possession of the drug.

Law professor Dan Howard, who led the commission of inquiry, believes that how the public money is being spent in New South Wales is completely unbalanced. One of the ideas in the report was that possession of small amounts of meth for personal use be entirely decriminalised. It was the headline measure that every news outlet chose to focus on and, when I catch up with him, fresh from presenting his findings to the country's media, I get the sense that he's a little tired of decriminalisation being the sole focus of such a wide-ranging report.

'Within hours of our report coming out, the New South Wales police minister, David Elliott, gave a press conference in which he said that the idea of decriminalising drugs was just ridiculous. That was the tone of his voice. There was no room for discussion whatsoever.'

So it should come as no surprise that the officers serving in the NSW Police had a similar attitude.

Dan says that finding political allies was hard as the cabinet itself was just absolutely deadlocked on responding in any meaningful way to the inquiry. David Elliott was one of the major hurdles. The report sat on a shelf, a political football continually kicked into the long grass for two and a half years, while conservative views were log-jamming any progress.

But something must have gotten through because the government eventually reached a compromise to spend more money on the proposals that related to health initiatives—more rehab, and more people in the workforce for drug and alcohol treatment. The overall response included a new allocation of $500 million to pay for those things. It was a significant effort to try to level the playing field. Although still way less than the $1.5 billion being spent on law enforcement.

'We pretty much took the view that police were getting plenty of money, but on the other hand we were hearing from all the NGOs, the people who run rehabilitation units, all the harm-reduction and treatment side of things, that they were really struggling. Hardly any money was being spent on that at all in comparison to what was being spent on supply reduction through law enforcement.'

I wonder if Dan is frustrated by how many police officers have had the kind of Damascene conversion that Mick Palmer described, when the guys still on the frontline are stuck in the same old mindset.

'He's a good guy, a sensible man,' Dan says of Mick. 'But many serving police worry that there just isn't the support in place, the facilities to send people to when they encounter them.'

Despite their commitment to more health-related spending, the NSW government stopped short of accepting Dan's proposal to decriminalise methamphetamine. He says that he wasn't very surprised and had already floated the idea of a diversion scheme as a more palatable alternative to all-out decriminalisation. Under this proposal, a user caught with drugs can be diverted to a health intervention twice. If it happens a third time, they can be prosecuted.

'So look, I've spoken to our Labor politicians. I've spoken to the leader of the opposition and his cabinet, and they're very supportive. And I suspect that if they get elected, the whole attitude could change.'

At the time of writing, the Labor Party had indeed been elected to government in New South Wales, so time will tell if Dan's predictions come to fruition. If he's right, the state, indeed the country, could be taking its first tentative steps towards a soft decriminalisation of drug possession, albeit via the back door, introduced more gradually to avoid any inflammatory headlines that might suggest they were going 'soft on drugs'. But the reality is that no longer will users be smashed with the full force of the law for simply possessing drugs. At least not the first couple of times. It seems like full decriminalisation for possession is a much smaller step from that position, so who knows what could happen after that.

Dan is optimistic. He says that the pursuit of targets—cops trying to hit a certain number of arrests, year after year—has acted as a counterbalance to any moral or intellectual progress. He also believes that policing has shown a distinct lack of compassion. Sniffer dogs at music festivals are a great example.

Kieran is a professional music producer and promoter. He currently works for a company that organises some of the country's premier music festivals, which is why, when he turned up at Splendour in the Grass near Byron Bay in July 2018, he had a guest-list pass. He split from his friends, who had to take the other queue, and joined the line to access the site. He says that his jaw dropped when he saw what was waiting for him.

The guest-list line had been targeted by the NSW Police drug teams. Forty cops with a dozen dogs were walking along the line, the dogs working their way between revellers, poking their noses into crotches and bags, sniffing for narcotics. When one of the dogs stopped briefly next to Kieran, he was pulled out of the queue for questioning.

In a separate tented area, away from the entrance, a police officer informed Kieran that he had been identified by the dog as potentially carrying a banned substance. Kieran immediately and freely admitted that he had a pre-rolled cannabis cigarette in his pocket and produced it for them to inspect.

'That's when things got hectic for me,' Kieran tells me, clearly still a little distressed about his experience. 'The cop just told me that now they had to strip-search me.'

Kieran was taken outside to a grassy area and told to remove his coat and shirt, and to pull his trousers and underwear down to his ankles. As it was July, he remembers the cold as he lay out his possessions on the grass, but mostly he remembers the humiliation.

'They told me to lift my testicles so they could see under my scrotum,' he says. 'Then they made me pull back my foreskin so that they could see under there too.'

It's hard to imagine what quantity of drugs Kieran could have been storing inside his foreskin. The police officer's request seems more designed to cause him discomfort than to genuinely further the search for contraband.

'It was completely dehumanising,' Kieran remembers. 'I was crying, I was alone, and I felt like I was being sexually assaulted.'

For the crime of carrying a single marijuana cigarette, Kieran was written up and had to attend court the next day. He received a deferral of a criminal sentence in return for observing a six-month good behaviour bond. His legal fees came to more than a thousand dollars and, as part of his legal defence, his lawyer recommended that he 'kiss the boot'.

'I said that I was seeing a therapist to help me with my drug use, that it was a mistake and that I hadn't taken drugs since,' Kieran says. 'None of which is true, but that is what they said I had to do.'

Kieran still smokes weed. He says that alcohol doesn't agree with him so he finds a cannabis joint helps him to relax in the evening or at the weekend. He's a bright, charismatic, university-educated professional with a promising career ahead of him. He laughs when he tells me how the irony is that he's fastidiously health conscious. Like most of his generation, he exercises regularly, eats healthily, and is considerate of the planet and the environment. Kieran is not a threat to society.

'It's hard for me, when I've been treated so disproportionately, to see the police as people I can rely on ever again,' Kieran says.

When he was in the NSW Upper House, Greens MP David Shoebridge—since elected as a senator in federal parliament—released figures that showed NSW Police had paid no less than $20 million a year in out-of-court settlements to people wrongly searched, held and arrested by its officers. Shoebridge called these 'hush money' payments. Over the five years for which he obtained data, 2016 to 2020, more than 1000 victims were paid off and required to sign non-disclosure agreements as part of their settlement package. Not only is this evidence that the police are systematically overstepping their mandate, but it appears that they are paying money to stop anyone finding out about it.

'It's awful,' Dan Howard says when I relay Kieran's story to him. 'We recommended that all that sort of conduct needed to stop. But that was one of the things that they immediately rejected when the report first came out, without any discussion or any analysis of the report or its findings. The health minister and police minister just said, "No, we're not doing that, the police see that as a really important tool." Honestly. It's crazy. It's a very old-fashioned approach.'

'Old-fashioned' seems an understatement. The policy of targeting drug users at events where drugs are being consumed seems at odds with an intelligent society, never mind a compassionate one. People take drugs at music festivals. This is a fact of life in countries around the world and it will never stop, no matter how many sniffer dogs you throw at it. How many tens if not hundreds of thousands of dollars are being wasted on arresting, charging and trying people like Kieran who are no threat to society?

The answer unfortunately comes down to money. Current regulations require organisers of public events such as music festivals to pay privately for the cost of policing them. But they have no discretion over what policing they are deemed to require. If the police insist you have sniffer dogs, then you have to pay for them. The NSW Police even publish a shopping list: the price of an officer is stated at $139.90 per hour and a dog at $26.60. If you want your event to happen, you have to pay the cops and their dogs to 'protect' you. This literal protection racket adds tens of thousands of dollars to the bill, which is passed on to punters. Want to listen to your favourite band? Well, you need to pay the police to protect you from yourself, then.

I'm not surprised that the police argue that this revenue stream is important to them. Ironically, they probably need it to help pay off their legal bills and cover the hush money they pay to the people they harass and search illegally.

I wonder where Dan gets his optimism from. How does he remain upbeat when he spent more than a year researching this subject in such depth, producing such considered, well-thought-through recommendations only for them to be dismissed out of hand by those who have so clearly failed to fix the problem with their own ideas?

'I think the pendulum's swinging back to a level of compassion,' he says. 'It's surprising that we have been as tough as we have on this issue of use and possession. I think politicians have scapegoated people who possess drugs for too long. They love the fact that twenty thousand people are arrested every year in New South Wales, but imagine if those resources were diverted to better use?'

I wonder if Dan is right. How we treat drug users is a cultural issue that swings from one position to the next as easily as fashion. The view that it is a crime to be in possession of drugs feels like it is now out of date, a function of a broken society that says, 'It's your fault that you've chosen to do this, so you need to accept the consequences.' Such a view lets governments off the hook and allows politicians to dodge responsibility. They can reject sensible policies that seek to mitigate harm and instead divert blame for their failures onto others. But while it may be easier to point the finger at others for a while, eventually the only person left to point at is yourself.

Dan and Mick both represent a new wave of progressive thinking on how we police drug use. They may be wrong, and their ideas may not work, but they have both earned the right to say that the status quo isn't working either. Don't they have a point? Who was it that said madness was doing the same thing over and over and expecting a different result? In that case, Australia is gripped by madness and needs help to see it.

———

What if we considered for a moment that users of drugs might not be the problem? In 2001, Portugal decriminalised the personal possession of all drugs as part of a wider reorientation of policy towards a health-led approach. Drugs are still confiscated if you're caught with them, and possession can result in an 'administrative fine', but users are largely no longer criminalised. The results have been encouraging. Drug-related deaths have remained below the EU average since the policy was introduced, the proportion of prisoners sentenced for drugs has fallen from 40 to 15 per cent, and rates of drug use have remained consistently below the EU average. Other places, including the US state of Oregon, have followed Portugal's example. Perhaps Australia could join that club?

Decriminalisation would not extend to suppliers of drugs. They should still be considered to be part of the problem, and treated accordingly. Portugal did not decriminalise drug trafficking and neither should Australia. If you're caught in Lisbon with more than a gram of ice, then you're usually considered a dealer, arrested, and face up to fourteen years in prison. In 2022, Portuguese law enforcement seized more than 15 tonnes of cocaine at its borders. But freeing up the money spent arresting and prosecuting users of drugs boosts the budgets of law enforcement agencies that target organised crime groups bringing the drugs in in the first place.

There are still grey areas. For example, the debate still needs nuance when considering what to do with users like Vix and Chris, who are turning to petty crime, producing and dealing to feed their own habits. To me, it seems harsh to see those behaviours as the real problem when set against the activities of suppliers importing Burmese ice by the tonne.

Vix, Chris and Rich are hustling to survive. Sure, you might not approve of their moral choices, but what is it we want? If we try to focus on the big picture, then the goal is to improve society and the experience of the people living in it. To do that, we need to stop wasting money on the whack-a-mole approach to demand reduction and focus instead on what people like Dan and Mick, those who've spent time at the coalface, living these issues day after day, are telling us. They are pointing us in a different direction, towards prioritising harm-reduction strategies for users, freeing up law enforcement resources to focus on the big wins in supply reduction, and allowing police officers to get back to policing our communities.

Supply reduction is an important tool of law enforcement. Shutting down super-labs run by Burmese militia groups and intercepting high-volume shipments coming in at the border is where significant dents can be made in the profits of criminal networks. Supply reduction should continue to target such operations but it can only improve our overall experience if engaged as part of a smarter strategy, one that stops wasting money on prosecuting small-time dealers and users, and starts instead to dovetail with harm-reduction strategies.

This is where I'd like to turn next: to ask what such a future might look like, and how we could all learn to live more easily in the knowledge that people around us are always going to choose to use drugs.

11

WHERE'S THE HARM?

So far, the Meth Road has taken me from the backstreets of Brisbane to the jungles of the Golden Triangle and back through the Gold Coast and Southport to the quiet seaside towns of the NSW Central Coast. Along the way, I've met cooks and smugglers, meth users and law enforcement, and I've developed a better understanding of the issues that these people face in their efforts to survive. Meanwhile, the inexorable flow of methamphetamine from Asia to Australia shows no sign of abating any time soon.

Reports of recent busts suggest that meth use continues to be prevalent at a level unseen anywhere else in the developed world. The impression I'm left with is that, by any measure, the current government strategy, at state and federal level, of trying to police our way out of trouble is failing miserably.

Some people are slowly coming around to the idea that things have to change. But change to what? I wonder what would happen if you asked ordinary Australians what they think. What do people want to see from their government's drug policy? If any of us could wave a magic wand and change one thing, what would that be?

I put this question to Julian, the Queensland cop whose thirty-year career put him at the forefront of anti-drug policing, raiding clandestine laboratories and shutting down organised crime groups. I asked him, as a police officer, what would he change either about political policy or police strategy that would make a positive difference. His answer was a little surprising.

'The only thing I'd change is I'd stop trying to legitimise cannabis,' he says. 'Because cannabis is the gateway drug to all other drugs. Nobody who's an ice addict now didn't use cannabis. They all start with cannabis.'

I'm surprised to hear a frontline police officer still talking this way, and when I put it to him that he could say the same thing about alcohol, or cigarette smoking, he flatly refuses to engage. In fact, he doubles down on cannabis being the problem, using expressions like 'thin end of the wedge' and 'important to send a tough message'. He does not accept that drug dogs and festival searches might be problematic, nor will he engage with the kind of evidence that we've explored in the previous chapters.

Julian makes me feel that whatever new solutions are needed, they're not going to come from within the police. Their faith in themselves, despite evidence to the contrary, is disappointingly myopic.

But while views like Julian's are disheartening, they are also understandable. Cognitive dissonance is quite common in situations where people are asked to accept that something they've been doing, dedicated their professional lives to, is actually hurting people. It's very hard to admit that, despite your best intentions, you've been making things worse. So instead, people like Julian make a blind commitment to buckling down and continuing with the same approach.

The police will always be a fundamentally important keystone of a functioning, civilised society and a vital part of its future. Whatever solutions others may offer, they will require the police to support them or they simply won't work. So the real question is not only 'What do Australians want?' but also 'What can the police buy into?'

I think it's fair to say that everyone accepts Australia has an ice-addiction issue. Like it or not, methamphetamine addicts exist everywhere in Australian society. I have spoken to users at all levels: lawyers, doctors, nurses, businesspeople, prostitutes, rough sleepers. As long as they are still using drugs, we need to better figure out how to make peace with them, because as we've seen, you can't lock them all up, rehab isn't a solution for everyone and the supply of drugs isn't stopping any time soon.

To get a better understanding of the public mood, I've taken a look at some of the polling data that's been gathered recently. Community polling is a curious beast. Polling done in the past by the research group Essential, for example, demonstrates the internally contradictory attitudes Australians have to drug law reform. A poll conducted in 2018 asked people whether they supported or opposed various drug policies. While 60 per cent supported (11 per cent opposed) pill-testing services at, say a music festival, where trained professionals could test and inform you how safe your drugs were to consume, 79 per cent of the same people supported the use of police sniffer dogs at the entrance to the music festivals to arrest people carrying drugs. Just 12 per cent of people were opposed.

My own view is that these data reflect a society that is very much in favour of doing something, but is also perhaps a little confused about what to do. We are unable to fully understand the policy issues in detail, which of course works in favour of dinosaurs like Julian, who lobby against changing the status quo. Politicians, too, might be aware of the evidence for change but are reluctant to take on the cops, so they prefer to just leave things as they are.

One of the more divisive policy options that seems to split people down the middle is the idea of creating regulated safe places where people are able to inject or inhale drugs under medical supervision. The Essential poll found 47 per cent in favour and 36 per cent against such a policy. In other similar polls, the numbers in favour drop when the question asks if the consumption room should be in the respondent's own postcode. To take a look for myself, I'm driving into Sydney to visit one of the very first government-run injecting rooms, established more than twenty years ago.

———

I approach Sydney from the west, driving over the Blue Mountains, along the highway into the city's suburbs. After passing by Sydney Olympic Park, I cross the Anzac Bridge into the congestion of the CBD and the epicentre of what is undoubtedly one of the world's most iconic cities. Around half of Sydney's 5 million inhabitants were born overseas. The largest diasporas are undoubtedly from East and South-East Asia. Nearly 20 per cent of Sydney residents speak an Asian language at home, a reminder of the country's close relationship with its nearest neighbouring continent.

Recent methamphetamine seizures at Sydney's port have discovered hundreds and hundreds of kilograms shipped from Asia inside blocks of marble, coconut-water bottles and electric barbecues. The gangs are becoming more and more ingenious, and every time I read of one of these busts, I imagine how many other shipments made it through unscathed. Sydney is probably the entry point for tonnes of meth annually.

No wonder then that the price of meth on the streets of Sydney is the lowest in the country. An eight ball (3.5 grams) typically goes for $500 here compared to $750 in Brisbane. As with most commodities, the closer you get to the source, or the port of importation, the cheaper the price.

The place that has long held the reputation for being the best spot for purchasing meth on the street is the Kings Cross district. Prior to the explosion of meth in Australia, Kings Cross was a longstanding hotspot for heroin use and therefore heroin overdoses. As the city saw in the early 2000s, ambulances were running up Darlinghurst Road around the clock, seven days a week, fifty-two weeks a year. The area was littered with dirty needles, people were injecting in doorways and dealers were openly selling in the street.

It was also a hotbed for prostitution, and budget hotel rooms were available to rent by the hour. People began renting rooms not for sex but just to have somewhere safe to inject. The local hotels started operating as quasi shooting galleries and the police, seeing that there was some benefit to taking drugs off the street, were happy to turn a blind eye.

The local community also recognised the benefits of taking the drugs off the street so that when they were offered a new official strategy, they took it seriously. Surveys of residents and businesses showed growing support for formally taking the injecting off the streets. The result was the country's first state-controlled injecting room, where users of intravenous drugs could safely go for their fix, without the threat of arrest, safe from the dangers of using dirty needles and out of sight of the wider community.

Occasionally, when a community commits to change and supports it wholeheartedly, amazing results can be achieved. Kings Cross is testament to that. In 2001, with government support, the Uniting Church oversaw the establishment of one of the world's first medically supervised injecting centres and now, twenty-two years later, well over a million drug injections have taken place within its walls, resulting in an 80 per cent reduction in ambulance call-outs in the area after the centre opened.

The centre is located on the main street, opposite the train station, next to a Thai restaurant. It's so inconspicuous that it could easily be mistaken for a GP surgery. When I arrive early in the morning, I'm invited in to take a look around by the centre's medical director, Dr Marianne Jauncey, who's been running the place for over fifteen years.

Dr Jauncey is a smiley, talkative woman who brims with enthusiasm and even a little pride as she tells me about her job and how successful the program has been. After spending so much time on this journey listening to stories that have less to celebrate, I find it a welcome relief to hear some good news.

Dr Jauncey says that she isn't personally religious but the support of the local Uniting Church was key to convincing the government to concede to trialling the centre initially. She says that over the years since, she's been able to see the complexity in many of the issues around meth use. Take, for instance, decriminalisation.

'I do believe in decriminalisation, of course,' she says. 'But to say that access plays no role in use is actually just wrong. It might be an inconvenient truth for some people, but it's still wrong.'

During the pandemic, Dr Jauncey says the centre saw significantly less heroin due to the shortage of the drug coming into the country, but gradually she says it's returned again to the same levels as pre-pandemic. That suggests that there weren't warehouses full of heroin that were ready to jump in to fill the gap in supply. Meth, on the other hand, she says was much more available, and so what they saw at the injecting rooms was meth use replacing heroin use. Her conclusions were that, first, meth supplies had been stockpiled prior to the border closures; second, that access to the drug was fundamental to use.

Dr Jauncey says that whether you're talking about legal or illegal drugs, usage is affected by regulation. If you advertise cigarettes to kids and then make them freely available, then use goes up. What we're learning from the explosion of cannabis legalisation in the US is that when you can buy cannabis in the form of oils, vapes and gummy bears, the use of the drug goes up.

Interestingly, she says that one of the things the centre monitors is the relationship between meth use and violence in the area. During the period post-pandemic, when meth use went up, there was no associated uptick in violent incidents. This is at odds with people's fears about what happens when somebody uses ice.

'Are you going to be frightened of me if I'm holding a glass of wine or beer?' Dr Jauncey asks me cryptically. 'No, but you're going to think it's pretty odd at ten past nine in the morning on a workday. Whereas if I've got an ice pipe and said I'm using methamphetamine, many people will back away because they have this idea that I am automatically, inevitably a violent, crazed, psychotic individual. And it's just not true. Alcohol is associated with violence in some people some of the time. Methamphetamine use is associated with violence in some people some of the time.'

This point about location and context is really important. I can think about the last wedding I went to and how drunk pretty much everyone at it was. We were all dancing, talking loudly, probably telling the same story three times in a row. It's quite shocking how normalised that kind of behaviour is in that particular context but, if we took one of the people from that wedding out of that scenario and transplanted them to their local main street at eight o'clock in the morning, how terrifying they would seem to other people. If I saw myself in that state in that context, I'd give myself a very wide berth and say, 'My God, that person is off their head.'

If we think about drugs in the same way we think about alcohol, then we might end up with very different opinions. Usually, if I ask somebody who has decided that all drugs are bad, 'Do you drink alcohol?', the answer is often 'Oh, but that's different.'

Why is it different? Because it's legal? Well, what about if I legalised all of the other drugs? Would that make it the same?

'You can't do that,' is the common refrain. Why? 'Because they're all bad.'

And round we go. Yet, we can all see that alcohol causes harm, that it leads people into a dissociative state, that it results in violence, unsafe driving, domestic abuse, ruined lives and so on. And yet, not only do we accept alcohol but we celebrate it. Australia is a country that I would say wholeheartedly endorses the view that it is positively un-Australian not to drink. The NSW premier's first photograph post-lockdown was taken in a pub—drinking a beer.

Many people in Australia would feel confronted—threatened, even—if they were to encounter someone injecting drugs in a public place. Yet people who want to consume alcohol are provided with so many private places to go—there's a pub in every town. It seems reasonable to ask why we couldn't also provide places for people to inject illegal drugs.

Australia currently has only two places where people can inject drugs under supervision: the centre in Kings Cross and a second in Melbourne. The Kings Cross centre has been evaluated independently about a dozen times with overwhelmingly positive findings over the last twenty years.

So why, when the need to do something new is so great and the benefits of the centre are so well documented, has Australia failed to establish more than one other medically supervised injecting centre in twenty years?

There is momentum growing for a US-style type of decriminalisation of cannabis in many countries, including Australia, right now. Yet, to me, it seems a little wrong-headed to consider decriminalising the drugs that do the least harm. We're saying that the less harmful a drug, the more we should look at decriminalising it, when there's actually an argument for saying the opposite.

Many people, like Kieran, use cannabis for fun. But what about the people for whom it's really a health issue because they've become dependent in their use, where use is now problematic because they're homeless, they've got schizophrenia, they've got post-traumatic stress disorder, they've got hepatitis C? Isn't that where we should treat use as a health issue? Aren't these the people in most need of help? Isn't this where we most need to decriminalise use in order to allow those people to get that help?

That line of reasoning is not where people naturally go. Instead, we tend to think first about the harms and therefore the need to send a message to people to avoid the harms. But actually the real message we're sending by criminalising use is that, if you are really in trouble with your drug use, you can't put up your hand and ask for help. The response of a civilised society to that request should be to support you, not criminalise you.

Now I don't believe, like Karly does, that everybody has a God-given right to access whatever drug they want. That is not my world view. But I do believe that if somebody is in trouble, they absolutely deserve care. People who ask for help deserve access to high-quality, non-stigmatising health care.

In Australia, it takes on average eighteen years from someone showing the first sign of problematic drug use to them ending up in treatment. That is a terrifying statistic. Because the sad truth is that it takes so long because of stigma, because of shame and because of the law. So to me, I would actually say one of the problems about decriminalising cannabis is you risk perpetuating the 'othering' that says *these* drugs are okay, while *those* drugs are the problem. *These* users are good people, but *those* users are bad people. I think they all deserve support, care and treatment.

'The stigmatising and the moralising does so much harm,' Dr Jauncey says. 'People don't continue to use drugs because it's fun. Acute withdrawal is ugly. You feel like you've been hit by a bus and while you're not going to die purely and simply from withdrawal, heavens above, you feel like you are.'

What's the one thing that someone in withdrawal can do to instantly find relief from that pain? Something that will make all the horrible symptoms go away? Start using again. One more hit and you can kick the can down the road, which is why it's so very hard to give up.

In the meantime, Dr Jauncey and her team want to ensure that users stuck in this painful spiral get the care and protection that they need to stay alive. After registering at the front desk, users are called through to a room where they are provided with clean syringes and needles. Users are invited to sit in individual cubicles, not unlike those in an open-plan office, where their 'desk' is equipped with a safe disposal box for the syringe after use. In case of anyone having an adverse reaction to the drugs, there is a treatment room where they can receive emergency care.

The centre has strict rules so that all its patrons must be over eighteen, not pregnant or already intoxicated, and have already injected drugs in the past. The majority of registered users are regular visitors (at least once a week), and about half are there to inject meth. Once they've taken their hit, they move into another room where they can sit for a while. This is where Dr Jauncey and her team can offer them support, whether that might be treatment or counselling.

'This is about positive change,' she says. 'About being client-centred and meeting someone where they're at. I'm not going to push treatment on you if it's not what you want or need right now because that's not going to work. But if I'm having a conversation with you and you are talking about how tired you are and how sick of everything you are, and it sounds like you've had enough, then I can offer help.'

She says that only happens because she has earned the trust and acceptance of the people she wants to help. The room has a book where visitors can write comments on their experiences. Dr Jauncey says that the feedback is all too often heartbreaking because it merely reflects the relief people feel at having been treated like a human being for the first time in a long time. She shows me an example from only the day before. It reads: 'Thank you for treating me like a human today.'

'Great,' she says. 'Because I'm part of a health system that apparently doesn't.'

————

When the injecting rooms were first considered by the government, the reservations that were levelled at the plans included fears that the centre would attract drug users to the area, send out a message that drug use was being condoned, become a hub for drug dealing, and draw in social low-lifes that residents didn't want to have roaming their streets. None of those things happened.

The argument that drug users, even users of meth-amphetamine, are bad people breaks down when you start talking to them. I've seen, over the course of my journey across Australia, that most users have some form of trauma, often institutional, in their past. Too often, it has seemed like their drug use has been a form of self-medicated therapy, a way to help deal with the fallout, the lasting damage caused by that abuse.

There is so much institutional complicity involved in the bad experiences that users have described, often resulting in chronic unemployment, homelessness and mental illness, that I don't think can be seen as separate from society.

I feel any reasonable person might ask themselves, 'Is the blame for that neglect not at society's door already?' Where is the accountability for that? Because the consequences are quite real for the victims, and the lived-experience stories that I've heard are shocking when set against the extreme levels of stigmatisation that these people face every day in Australian society.

The media has a very big part to play in this. My colleagues and I in the fourth estate have difficult questions to answer. When health care professionals like Dr Jauncey describe how people on methamphetamine are treated as wild animals instead of as human beings, then we need to ask ourselves to what extent we have been complicit in creating the impression that that is appropriate. These stereotypes that we see in the press, on the television, of people smoking a pipe and then turning into an out-of-control Incredible Hulk character don't come out of thin air. Such narratives take root in the public consciousness because the media put them there.

Attitudes can change. Look at mental ill-health and how it was widely stigmatised prior to the last decade. Since then, the stigma of being someone with a mental health issue has really reduced. We've started to deal with how we think of people with mental health problems in a much more compassionate and intelligent way. People are able to talk about it more openly, more government money is being spent on treating it, and every television or news item that has anything to do with suicide or mental health always has a message at the end—a helpline where there will be trained people waiting to help you to talk about how you're feeling. There are some wonderful initiatives going on now that were unthinkable even fifteen years ago.

I could liken our collective attitude to how mental health was viewed back then. The implication is that we can change our attitudes in the same way if we make the same amount of effort and try to show the same understanding and compassion. It's going to take some time because of all the residual stigmatisation and old-fashioned, judgemental attitudes shown by politicians like David Elliott and police officers like Julian. These men claim to be part of the moral majority when, in fact, they're the opposite—they're the dregs of an old guard that sees punishing people for how they deal with trauma as a means to holding on to their own power and influence. It's time for them to move aside and let people with fresh ideas have a turn at the crease.

———

Destigmatising drug use is possible in a society. When it's done right, it can have very measurable benefits. To provide an example, I want to look at how attitudes to another type of amphetamine, MDMA are being challenged by people in the UK whose lives have been tragically affected by the drug. Their goal is simple—to save lives.

Dan was sixteen when he and a bunch of friends went to a rave in the UK. His mother, Fiona, had no idea that was where he was going because her son had lied to her, saying that he was going to a friend's party. She had no reason to disbelieve him because Dan was a good kid. He was doing well at school, and Fiona describes him to me as an 'incredibly nice person, funny, interesting and a complete chatterbox'.

The rave was being held in a warehouse on an industrial estate miles from the family home so Dan and his mates took a train, picking up two and a half grams of MDMA on the way. They shared out the drugs before they got there, four of the boys splitting two single-gram bags, while Dan took a third bag that contained the extra half-gram. They all dissolved the powder in bottles of water and as they neared their stop, maybe fearing that he'd be searched on his way into the venue, Dan downed his bottle in one.

'If he'd only sipped it like everybody else, he would probably have picked up how strong it was,' Fiona says. 'But he didn't know.'

The dose that Dan took proved to be lethal. The post-mortem didn't show that Dan had a particular sensitivity to MDMA, only that the drug had overwhelmed his young body and his temperature soared to 42 degrees Celsius. At this temperature, the body's organs can't cope and they shut down. Dan was rushed to hospital at 4.30 a.m. An hour later, Fiona got a knock on the door from the police. Despite the best efforts of the medics, Dan died two days later.

Nobody is sure why exactly Dan died. Maybe his bag actually contained a gram, not half a gram. Maybe his drugs came from a different batch. The police weren't able to do toxicology on the drugs because there weren't any left.

I wonder if, given the option, Dan might have tested his drugs. Fiona thinks he would.

'Oh gosh, Dan would've done, yeah,' she says. 'I'm absolutely sure that if drug checking was available, he would've taken that up, and then he'd have known.'

Since her son's death, Fiona has founded a charity that aims to educate young people about drugs. She has also formed an alliance with The Loop, a drug-testing charity, who set up centres in places where young people take drugs. She says that her first experience of seeing The Loop in action was at a music festival.

'There were a bunch of kids in there who had all kinds of nonsense going on in their heads,' she remembers. 'They put it down to there being some bad pills going around. So they were able to look after them and warn everyone else.'

It's hard to see how a scheme like this sends 'the wrong message', as Julian the Queensland cop thought it did. To me, the message that there's a batch of bad pills going round that could harm you if you ingest them is exactly the *right* message.

Fiona says that the most important aspect to her own work is educating young people, aged eleven to fifteen, about drugs. 'We do it in a very careful way,' she says about her presentation style. 'Because we know that the majority of kids won't ever use drugs, but that a significant minority will. We don't want to project behaviours onto people or normalise anything, so we come at it sideways, talking about what to do if a friend is taking drugs.'

There is so much to understand in terms of the risks for young people getting into drugs, and a lot of work to be done around their decision making and understanding, especially in the social environments where decisions about drugs and alcohol are made.

But there is always going to be a degree of unpredictability unless those people can also have a conversation about the likely impact of those decisions. That conversation may be the first honest conversation a young person has ever had about drugs, the first time they have really asked, 'What does this mean and what's going on for me that means I'm doing this?'

The truth is that recreational drug use—including of methamphetamine—will continue to occur in all sections of society. Dan's story may be about MDMA and not meth but it shows us that even 'good kids' use hard drugs recreationally. If we want to reduce the risks, then they need to be educated. And even then, many will still choose to take hard drugs, so the focus has to be on how to keep them safe despite this decision.

'Recently, we are hearing a lot more about contaminated meth,' says Cameron Francis, CEO of The Loop in Australia. 'The meth people have been using has something else in it but they're not sure what.'

The Loop's testing suggests that Cameron may be describing N-isopropylbenzylamine, an isomer of methamphetamine which has been used in the past to adulterate meth. N-isopropylbenzylamine looks just like ice but it causes side effects such as headaches and confusion. A recent study published by Ningbo University sounded an alarm about its potential long-term toxicity in meth users.

Cameron says that another fear he has is that the synthetic opioid, fentanyl, will soon start turning up in Australian meth, as it's already doing in the United States with fatal consequences. He thinks that it's only a matter of time and makes an even stronger case for more drug-testing centres in Australia.

Interestingly, as mentioned earlier, 60 per cent of Australians support the idea of drug-testing centres at music festivals, while 79% support the use of police sniffer dogs at music festivals. This maybe also offers a glimpse into where the Australian public are in terms of drugs policy.

This seems strange to an outsider. There are so many elements of Australian society that seem to be overgoverned and overpoliced. The image that Australia presents to the world—that it is a laidback, progressive place whose people take a relaxed approach to life—is quite different from my experience. There seems to be a real contradiction between the anti-authoritarian narrative and a society that welcomes such stringent policing.

Cameron sees hope in recent polling. 'It's only 13 per cent that said they oppose [drug] testing,' he says, quoting research that The Loop commissioned last year. So the opposition is soft. But public support doesn't always translate into policy change, so if drug testing is to be introduced in Australia as it has been in the UK, the lawmakers need to change their attitudes. The 'sending the wrong message' argument is woefully out of date and out of touch. The need to reduce harm has never been greater, and organisations such as The Loop and the Kings Cross injecting rooms can help massively in achieving positive results and saving lives.

———

I think meth is too destructive a drug to fully legalise it. I just can't see how that would work in a civilised society that seeks to protect and serve its citizens. But I do think that decriminalising users is a good idea. Even if you think meth is bad, taking the view that users of meth are not bad is the only way forward. 'Out with sniffer dogs, in with drug testing and safe injecting places' seems a clear and positive expression of such a thought.

Decriminalisation has wrongly become the sole focus of the debate. I think that it is an important component of a new way forward but only when it is combined with the kind of harm-reduction strategies we have discussed here.

Rehumanising meth users seems to me to be a vital first step, and something that most people could buy into.

There's a debate among some progressive thinkers in Australia about whether a portion of the demand for methamphetamine could be met by other drugs like MDMA. The idea is that if there was a regulated supply of MDMA, then we could replace meth use, especially in young users, who might prefer something less destructive and shorter acting, and where one dose doesn't take away your whole weekend and leave you itching for more. It's an interesting idea but one that would need to be backed by either a regulated supply or widely available drug testing if we're not to repeat the tragic experience that Fiona and her family had to suffer. I'm not sure that Australia is ready for such a progressive move just yet.

In the meantime, a greater focus on harm reduction is part of the wider change that's needed. It's going to take a huge attitude shift on the part of government and the police, but only if the people get behind it will the lawmakers find the confidence to do it. All the research suggests that a more humane approach to addiction can generate changes that benefit everybody in society, so why not try it? The current plan isn't working—is it?

EPILOGUE

THE END OF THE ROAD

I'll admit that, at first, I found Australia's relationship with methamphetamine shocking. I was also surprised to discover that Australia is way more socially conservative than many people like me think it is. Australians have garnered a reputation internationally for having built one of the most pragmatic societies in the developed world; once Australians make their minds up to do something, they do it and they don't care what other people think. This strong single-mindedness is perhaps what is needed now to solve an undoubtedly critical and unique problem.

The tide certainly seems to be turning. Centre-left federal and state governments are now in every parliament except Tasmania, which makes me feel like there is a moment here, a point when some meaningful progress might be made on drug policy. Recent political shifts in those state parliaments suggest there's finally an appetite for moving towards a more progressive agenda when it comes to drug law reform. This chance should not be missed.

First up is the decriminalisation of possession and use of drugs in Australia. As we've seen already in chapter ten, New South Wales is the last state to be moving towards decriminalisation, albeit by the back door. Even conservative Queensland has announced it intends to introduce a 'three strikes and you're out' criminal diversion scheme, where people caught with a small amount of drugs will escape criminal conviction and be diverted into health programs. This is good news.

But there is more to be done. Over the last three years, I've been consumed by thinking about methamphetamine and I have made certain observations based on my experiences which I want to share. This is not meant to be preachy. It's not a dogmatic manifesto but rather some fresh ideas that seem to me to be worth considering. I'm looking forward to debating them with people who either agree or disagree with some or all of them.

The question that I opened this book with was 'What do Australians want?' The conclusion that I've come to is 'Something different'. We'll get onto what exactly that might be in a minute but let's all first acknowledge what it is not. Nobody wants what has gone before—a fifty-year-long 'war on drugs' that has been resoundingly lost, and is no longer fit for purpose. I could liken it to the war in Vietnam, which also cost lives, which went on for far too long, which ultimately had to be scrapped to the history books and looked back on unfavourably. Now, like then, the time has come to make peace.

This is not surrender. I am not suggesting that we throw up our hands and accept that everyone be allowed to take whatever drugs they want whenever and wherever they desire. I am not arguing that methamphetamine be legalised, not even that its supply be decriminalised. Rather, I am saying that it is time to renew and refresh the way that we deal with its now inevitable presence in society.

Make no mistake, my firm view is that methamphetamine is unlike any other drug that is available in Australia. Meth is not a recreational drug like cannabis or ecstasy or even cocaine. If anything, it more closely resembles heroin or crack cocaine in terms of its addictiveness and health impact, but still is more destructive than either.

Methamphetamine has a frightening power to destroy minds and, in the process, destroy lives. Its unique pharmacological method, which floods the brain with dopamine and keeps it there for such a long time, makes it malignant, insidious and toxic. When I began writing this book, I naively thought that at some point I would give it a try, go gonzo and smoke a pipe with some users on the streets of Bangkok or Brisbane just to see what it was 'really' like. But when I saw up close how methamphetamine affected users, I changed my mind.

I have no problem admitting that I have, in the past, taken drugs. I've enjoyed the effects of some narcotics in recreational situations. These days, I drink alcohol socially and very occasionally smoke cannabis but I have no desire to ever take methamphetamine. I want no part of it.

But does that give me the right to legislate for others? I don't think so. I think that everyone has the right to make those choices for themselves. However, I also think that society has a responsibility to serve and protect its people. There is the rub. We need to accept that meth has many undesirable societal side effects that drugs like ecstasy/MDMA and cannabis don't have, while at the same time safeguarding the people who take meth and the people who encounter them while they do.

In many ways, the dangers of meth more closely resemble those of alcohol than any other drug: a dissociative state, use lasting for days and weeks, problematic social behaviours like violence and psychosis, and so on. I think that if you invented alcohol today, no government in the world would legislate its use.

But it is important that we separate the drug from the user. I can say that I think meth is a bad drug but that is not the same as saying people who use meth are bad people. Society belongs to us all and, as such, we all should be served and protected by it. The solution, as with most things, lies in how we compromise and innovate so as to best accommodate everyone.

So I have reached a few conclusions for specific areas of policy that I think could be addressed in order to improve how methamphetamine affects us all.

SUPPLY

INTELLIGENCE GATHERING

Limiting the amount of meth coming into Australia is always going to be a difficult strategy to make work on its own. The Chinese successfully shut down production in China only for it to pop up in Myanmar. Shut it down in Myanmar and it will likely pop up in Mexico or Afghanistan instead. To an extent, that means it might always feel like a fool's errand, and that as long as the demand is there, the supply will find a way. But it's also my belief that unbridled supply would reduce street prices in Australia to such an extent that we could see a surge in consumption, which would be worse.

That said, if we're going to pursue supply reduction as a strategy, then it needs to be smarter and more intelligence led. More undercover work is necessary if we are to have better knowledge of who and where the biggest suppliers are operating within Myanmar. We need to have a better understanding of what exactly is going on in the corners of the Burmese jungle where armed groups and illicit drug gangs operate.

When I have spoken to Australian Federal Police agents, they're always in their bureaus in Yangon, Bangkok or Beijing. None of them seem ever to have been to Shan State themselves. That's not to say that the agents in Bangkok and Yangon and Beijing don't play an important role but they're essentially diplomatic functions. They're senior people based out of an embassy, which means they can liaise directly with other senior people on the Myanmar or Chinese sides. This function is really important but it's a completely different function from the intelligence function.

Nothing beats getting out and having your boots on the ground. My own experiences tell me that it's dangerous to rely on secondhand intelligence, especially when it's coming from drug dealers and war combatants. Sometimes, the intelligence making its way out of Myanmar is credible. But in a market where everybody is a potential bad actor, and where many have openly said to me that they bleed intelligence to the authorities to screw over their rivals and gain a competitive advantage, I feel like the AFP are playing too passive a role.

Of course, running intelligence in someone else's country is tricky. You can do it openly with their permission, but that's difficult when you're dealing with a military junta. Or you run covert intelligence operations, which you could do, for example, along the Thai and Lao borders, but that requires a big investment in covert agents and running criminal sources.

But if one of the main goals is supply reduction, then the targets must be those who are operating the meth labs. It is possible that the AFP have some covert operations going on that they just don't talk about, but when I've asked this question the answer seems always to be that it's just not possible. If this is true, I think this shows a lack of imagination and ambition.

The AFP officers sitting in offices in Beijing or Yangon have to get out there and see what's going on for themselves. This is not impossible. If I can walk into the jungle and meet smugglers and cooks then it shouldn't be beyond the scope of the law enforcement and intelligence communities to do the same.

DIPLOMACY WITH CHINA

The fact that the Burmese military junta has been allowed to seize power, terrorise its people and enrich its generals is an international scandal. The resulting civil war now means that large swathes of the country are no longer under the sovereign control of the central government. This also poses a difficult question for the international community.

The MO of Burmese meth producers—or, at least, meth producers operating within Myanmar—is dependent on exploiting the secrecy created by the ongoing armed conflict. But in order to turn off the meth taps, we need first to be able to negotiate in those areas where meth is being produced. This requires a multipronged diplomatic approach.

Ultimately, the political situation in Myanmar may never resolve itself. We have to get more involved because Myanmar's problems have become Australia's problem. Policy needs to move beyond criminal justice responses to the supply side, and really grapple with the political and conflict factors supporting production in Myanmar. This ultimately is what could dent the output from the biggest supplier of Australia's meth. To get this policy to work, there is one key international player that Australia needs to bring on board: China.

It seems that every time we discuss the nefarious actions of bad actors in Asia, the elephant in the room is China. Ten years ago, I wrote about deforestation happening on an industrial scale in northern Laos, which was being conducted by Chinese companies who thought they were beyond the law. At the time, I found the barefaced denial by Chinese authorities of something that I had seen with my own eyes staggering but it helped me to understand that sometimes, the Chinese Communist Party (CCP) engages a different moral compass from that of governments in developed democracies.

Time and again, Chinese foreign policy seems to demonstrate how Beijing doesn't really care about how its policies affect the internal social fabric of other countries, let alone the human rights of its own citizens. On the contrary, the CCP are deliberately hands-off, engaging in plausible deniability, avoiding responsibility as much as they can.

But let's address some facts. First, China's borders are not 'porous', as is sometimes claimed. People, goods and narcotics are not flowing into China unregulated. During Covid, China exercised one of the most stringent border control policies in the world, and yet the flow of precursor chemicals from China over the Myanmar border into clandestine laboratories in Wa and Shan states continues unabated. At the very least, China is guilty of wilfully turning a blind eye to its role in meth production on an industrial scale.

For the Chinese government, maintaining face on the international stage is highly important. We've seen how they so effectively kicked the meth labs out of their own territory during the purges that took place between 2014 and 2017. It's time to work with them to help do the same in Myanmar.

One of the levers we have is to call them out publicly and shine a light on how Chinese factories are involved in the meth trade. This is one surefire way to get Beijing to act. Another is to work behind the scenes to identify where our common strategic goals could align. China has recently begun to publicly put pressure on Yangon to bring an end to the fighting within Myanmar. If these diplomatic signals are genuine then disrupting the cash flow of rebel militias would help with that. Meth is helping to fuel the war in Myanmar, so if China is serious about peace, there are ways in which we can help with that.

THE WA

Myanmar is still a sovereign nation and therefore its borders should be internationally recognised. But we need to have an honest debate about what to do with those territories that it no longer controls and may never do again.

The most important of these is Wa, where the Myanmar military and therefore the Myanmar state have completely lost control. The Wa, now governed by the UWSP and their army the UWSA, is operating as a quasi-independent narco-state, whose involvement in methamphetamine production is having a direct negative impact on not only Australia but several other countries in the region as well.

Action against Wa's production facilities in the form of US-style drone strikes wouldn't be effective, given the thick cover offered by the jungle canopy, but if there was a way for Australia and China to cooperate then targeted action against the Wa's laboratories could be to everyone's advantage.

Sooner or later, Wa has to be taken seriously. If they are indeed to become an independent state, then they need to play by the same rules and suffer the same consequences as everyone else.

SMUGGLING

Another area in which we can work with China as well as other Asian governments to great effect is by addressing the continuing existence of self-governing casino towns in the Golden Triangle. I'm talking about towns like Kings Romans and Mong La. These places are mind-blowingly problematic because, effectively, drug lords and gangsters have been handed their own mini countries, which allows them to act in ways that cause harm to the rest of the world. This is madness.

We need to put pressure on Laos and China to shut these guys down. When Laos last leased land to gangsters inside its territory, it was a town on the Chinese border called Boten.

The minute that Boten was seen as being contrary to China's national interest, its gambling and prostitution industries were shut down, and the people involved were chased out of town. Boten is now being rejuvenated with new luxurious hotels, shopping malls and a central business district. This is proof of what can be done. Without places like Kings Romans acting as staging posts and warehousing for smuggling operations, as well as money-laundering centres for billion-dollar drug enterprises, organised crime groups will find it much harder to act.

Thailand is our greatest ally in the South-East Asian region and there is a lot of political goodwill there to support supply-reduction strategies. In many ways, Thailand is stuck in the middle of a problem of someone else's making. The war to the north of its border is beyond its control, while the drugs that flow from it are taking as much of a toll on Thai society as they are on Australian society.

In 2021, Thailand spent US$133 million on suppressing drug-trafficking activities across its borders. This strikes me as an area in which Australia could help. There are currently proposals to cooperate more directly with Thai intelligence through the Five Eyes shared intelligence alliance of Australia, New Zealand, Canada, the UK and the USA. This is to be commended.

In return, the Thai authorities have to start arresting more people. It's no good intercepting 200 kilos of ice if you arrest none of the people who are trafficking it. Meth costs next to nothing in Myanmar so the cost of a border seizure is next to nothing for the gangs producing it.

The Phamuang have been effective in culturing relationships with criminal informants but using them to generate intelligence that leads to confiscation is only half the solution. The Phamuang must put pressure on CIs to share intel on who is pulling the strings further up the chain. I'm confident that, with help from the Five Eyes, we can quickly establish that those chains lead to senior people in the Wa and Shan armies and in the Tatmadaw, and maybe even to officials within China.

MEXICO AND AFGHANISTAN

The meth supply market is opening up. The cartels in Mexico can see how much money the Asian drug gangs make from methamphetamine in Australia and they are trying to muscle in. Last year a huge 1.8 tonnes of liquid meth bound for Melbourne was seized by authorities in Hong Kong. Its source is thought to be Mexico.

It's important to acknowledge that anything we do to interrupt Myanmar's meth supply routes will be seen as an opportunity by the cartels in Central and South America.

Reports from Afghanistan suggest that the Taliban could be next.

This makes an even stronger case to support the efforts of the AFP and the Australian Border Force in targeting large shipments from overseas. Making meth supply a riskier enterprise, while simultaneously shrinking demand, will make Australia a less attractive market to potential new entrants.

WHICH POLICE ARE THE BEST POLICE?

Supply reduction is not a game-ending solution but it can be effective. The data generated during the Covid years proves this. So the question is who is best placed to lead supply-reduction policy in Australia? I would argue that the data suggests that the actions of state police forces—the targeting of users and small-time dealers—is for the birds. Redirecting funds from state police to the AFP and border control makes far more sense if supply reduction is the goal.

This is not going to be popular with the police. But both state and federal governments need to get a grip. Who is in charge here? Moving funds away from policing may be initially unpopular with the electorate but politicians need to step up and make the argument in light of the evidence.

State police forces should be dealing with street crime, policing in the community, and locking up muggers and murderers. They have been proven to be relatively ineffective at interrupting drug supply at significant levels and so continuing to fund them in this area is a bad return on investment.

DRUG DOGS AND GAGGING ORDERS

The state police are also openly operating a quasi-security racket, forcing private events to hire police as security while knowingly targeting people who are no threat to society, often inappropriately searching and engaging in wider misconduct. The cost to the entertainment industry runs into the millions of dollars, while the police pay out further millions in hush money to those they've wronged.

The current policy is counterproductive. All the evidence shows that it does nothing but stigmatise, traumatise and criminalise a section of society that deserves better.

The issue of state police insisting that their victims sign non-disclosure agreements should also be banned. It is undemocratic for a state law enforcement agency to gag the very citizens it has failed to serve. People have a right to know when and how their police force has failed them and the police have a responsibility to stand up, face the criticism and explain how they can do better.

DEMAND

HARM REDUCTION

Harm-reduction strategies need full investment to make up the shortfall that has characterised years of overfunding police forces. Meth is bad but users of meth are not bad. Drug users need to be treated as human beings by our health care systems.

Proposals have been made to establish a second injecting room in Melbourne. This is a good idea and should be the start of a second wave of injecting rooms across the country. Objections to such plans are small-minded nimbyism and are not supported by the data.

Drug-testing facilities similarly need to be made more widely available. It might be sensible to trial their use at events where we know that drugs will be taken. For example, the money that music festivals save on sniffer dogs could be better channelled into drug testing.

I would bet on there being a marked reduction in hospitalisations and deaths as a result. Instead of young people necking all their drugs in one go when they see the police dogs, they can have them tested and plan how to consume them safely over the course of an event.

DECRIMINALISATION

It looks like there might finally be some public appetite for decriminalisation of drug use in Australia. Nearly every state seems to have embraced the concept of drug diversion courts whereby drug users will be given a second or even a third chance if they're caught with a small quantity for personal use. This is to be applauded.

Too much money and time has been wasted prosecuting drug users without seeing any reduction in use or supply. If there is no benefit to society and a limited pot of cash, then we should change tack and trial strategies that might actually benefit us rather than just pander to our prejudices.

What these new proposals offer is a country-sized trial of decriminalisation as a strategy. Even if it is happening through the back door, if proven successful and shown to effectively reduce crime and punishment costs without leading to increased drug use, then we'll have a mandate to expand it beyond the 'three strikes' format.

It's time to be practical and pragmatic. These are core Australian values on which intelligent policy can be built.

REHABILITATION

Australia's drug-rehabilitation system seems in crisis at just the time when it is most needed. Services are already massively oversubscribed while waiting lists get longer. Effectiveness is also being undermined by rogue actors entering the market and engaging in questionable practices.

A properly managed accreditation scheme is desperately needed. We've seen how delicate a user's rehabilitation experience can be. It doesn't work for everyone first time. Sometimes several attempts are necessary to get someone off drugs and back into being productive in society. But what is vital is that when someone asks for that help, the best care possible is available to them. These opportunities are precious and cannot be wasted.

Rehabilitation should be a vital cornerstone of the nation's drug policy and too important to leave to the free market to solve. Low barriers to entry expose the people who are asking for help to quasi-religious crackpots who think the earth is flat and that the moon landings were a hoax.

That's not to say that Christian-run rehab centres are all bad, but they do need to play by the same rules as everyone else. Science-led treatments by staff who are vetted and properly supervised should be mandatory. In Western

Australia, governments were actually funding a rehab centre performing exorcisms. Exorcisms and conspiracy theories are not what vulnerable people need; qualified therapy and empathetic case management are.

There is work underway to try to change the accreditation system for residential rehab centres but this needs to be stepped up. There's still too much exploitation and bad administration, even when the services are well intentioned.

Australia has a legacy of underfunded drug treatment to overcome. A lot of money is going to be needed to get it back to where it needs to be so it's heartening to see the NSW government earmark $500 million in extra funds for harm-reduction and treatment strategies as a result of Dan Howard's ice report. This is a good start.

OTHER DRUGS ARE AVAILABLE

There's an important question to explore around whether decriminalisation of less harmful drugs could cut down demand for more dangerous ones like meth.

Coming from the UK where cocaine is widely available, I can attest that meth is incredibly rare. This is despite having some major meth-producing hubs in nearby states like the Netherlands and Czech Republic.

It's certainly an interesting idea that a softer approach to other drugs in Australia could reduce meth use and therefore the harm caused by meth. But I'm not entirely convinced.

With regard to cocaine, Mexico's cartels arguably exact just as severe a toll on the Mexican people as the armed groups of Myanmar on the Burmese. How would we protect ordinary Mexicans from an expansion of Australia's cocaine supply?

Also, crack cocaine currently isn't a big problem in Australia. However, if cocaine was more available then crack use could easily become more widespread. I'm not convinced that swapping meth pipes for crack pipes is a great win for society.

Similar arguments could be made for opioids. However, having lived through a heroin epidemic, Australia may not have a great appetite for encouraging another one. And as for synthetic opioids like fentanyl, the experience of the US doesn't bode well for any country that experiences an increase in its availability. The US had almost 70,000 fentanyl-related overdose deaths in 2021.

I'm also not sure cannabis is a ready substitute for meth. It's possible that the demand for meth could be reduced by wider availability of MDMA—particularly for younger recreational drug users who could more safely use MDMA than meth in social situations like parties and festivals. But, as we've discussed, decriminalising MDMA would have to be done with great care. Pill testing would have to be made widely available at the same time to minimise potential harm.

———

I've travelled thousands of kilometres to research this book, and spoken to scores of people who are directly and indirectly involved in the meth trade in Asia and Australia. Over that time, I've changed my mind about a lot of things. I no longer see methamphetamine as just another recreational drug. I believe it to be a more corrosive narcotic than other 'party drugs' like cocaine and MDMA, and more destructive than heroin.

I've also seen how gangs are exploiting the political situation in Myanmar to make money from Australia's drug use. I saw how meth production and distribution in that country is contributing to a bloody civil war. Since the coup of 2021, more than one million people have been displaced in Myanmar, while the US-based conflict monitoring group ACLED have reported about 19,000 people have died. The military-led crackdowns on protests around the country have seen whole villages destroyed by military airstrikes, while militia-led mobs burn down civilian homes, forcing more and more people, in their desperation, to take up arms. But while the war has been bad for Myanmar, it has been good for the meth business.

Armed groups need money to fuel their struggle. The gangs behind the meth trade have been happy to oblige, providing the cash needed to buy bullets and guns in exchange for land in the jungle where they can cook meth, and provide safe passage across borders. Meanwhile young men and women die; children and families suffer. The people I remain in contact with in Shan State describe how life there is now fraught with danger. The 'days of democracy' are gone, they say. Shan has become a narco-state.

Yet the world turns a blind eye. Myanmar, a bit like North Korea, has become a 'buffer state'. It suits both West and East for Myanmar to remain the way it is, offering China and the West a bit of space from each other, while Russia sells the Burmese military arms with which to kill its people. All sides seem better served while

Myanmar remains a basket case, so we go on ignoring the plight of its people, because they are politically expedient on the international stage.

I care about injustice deeply. It's what has inspired me to travel all over the world calling out individuals, companies and governments who I see acting in ways that harm ordinary people who have no voice. Whether it's a US restaurant chain endangering the lives of indigenous people or governments disenfranchising citizens by riding roughshod over their human rights, I've tried my best to shine a light on bad behaviour. What is happening now in Myanmar is wrong. Were such a thing going on in a country nearer to the West—in Ukraine, for example—I think the reaction of the international community would be quite different.

Meanwhile, in Australia, there is injustice associated with the meth business too. Young men and women are dying here; it's just that the shooting is happening down a needle and not the barrel of a gun. There are hundreds of drug overdose deaths involving methamphetamine in Australia every year. Thousands of people are hospitalised, and tens of thousands more need drug treatment for problematic use. This situation is out of control and moving in the wrong direction.

The Meth Road is not a single track. It has many side roads and diversions, and the traffic changes route constantly, avoiding blockages and obstacles. But the flow is continuous and shows no sign of slowing down. Australia needs to adapt and take a more progressive path if it's going to effect meaningful change. The war on drugs in its current form has been lost. A new strategy will entail treating meth users as human beings rather than enemies to be defeated.

I have tried to humanise the people who make their living along the Meth Road, to put flesh on the facts and figures around methamphetamine. I think that the press and the government have behaved irresponsibly in their representation of methamphetamine users over the last decade with disastrous consequences. This vilification has stifled honest debate to such an extent that the public have developed skewed views about meth and the people who use it. I hope, in some way, I am helping to change that.

Yet I remain optimistic in spite of these considerable challenges. 'Why?' I might ask myself, when I think about how drugs generally and methamphetamine specifically will always be available, and that supply-reduction strategies will at best only stop the flood becoming an ocean. The answer lies with us. I think we can find a better way through improving our own attitudes about how we treat people who take drugs, and how we help those for whom drug use has become a problem. There is a more compassionate and caring solution to this problem than any previously tried and that is where we have the most to gain. Ultimately, the war on drugs has been lost. It's time to make peace and learn to live better with them.

ACKNOWLEDGEMENTS

Firstly, I'd like to thank everyone who appears in the book. I've changed many names and masked identities to protect people where I can, but you know who you are. Thank you all for sharing your stories with me. I hope that I have done you justice.

I am indebted to my publisher Tom Bailey-Smith at Allen & Unwin for his insightful edits. I'd also like to thank the rest of the team at A&U, including copyeditor Emma Driver, proofreader Pamela Dunne, publishing assistant Allegra Bonetto, Deborah Parry for her cover design, Mika Tabata for the map, Bella Breden for publicity and Shannon Edwards for marketing.

As always, my appreciation goes out to my indefatigable agent Gordon Wise at Curtis Brown. Thank you for believing in the book before anyone else and for your consistent support over the years.

To Sean Williams and Chen Chi Chang I'd like to say a big thank you for travelling many a mile with me along dark and dusty roads in pursuit of the 'white castle'. Your company made it all so much more enjoyable.

In Brisbane, I received invaluable support from Jennie Nicholl at the State Library. I'd like to thank Richard Horsey, John Coyne, Alessandro Rippa, Tom Kramer and Khuensai Jaiyen too for their expert input. Many thanks also to Michelle Thomas and Will Tregoning for helping to track down so many people with such rich and interesting stories to tell.

The biggest thank you of all, I save for Ruth Martin, the woman I met at the very start of this long road. Thank you for everything that you do, for everything we share. I couldn't have done it without you.